EDUCATING
WITH PURPOSE
THE HEART OF WHAT MATTERS

STEPHEN TIERNEY
Illustrations by Stan Dupp

First published 2020

by John Catt Educational Ltd,
15 Riduna Park, Station Road,
Melton, Woodbridge IP12 1QT

Tel: +44 (0) 1394 389850
Fax: +44 (0) 1394 386893
Email: enquiries@johncatt.com
Website: www.johncatt.com

ISBN: 978 1 913622 09 1

Set and designed by John Catt Educational Limited

Reflections on
Educating with Purpose

In this book, Stephen Tierney rightly focuses on the overall purposes of education – what matters, rather than just what works. *Educating with Purpose* invites us, as educators, to take a step back and look at the big picture about what we want from our schools and what we want for our children and young people. It raises issues of equity, social justice and community – and there has never been a more important time for these issues to be discussed.

Steve Munby, visiting professor, University
College London Institute of Education

At heart, this book is a reflection on why we invest in our children, which makes it relevant for school leaders, of course, but equally pertinent for teachers, governors, parents and anyone who wants to grapple with the reasons why we educate. Stephen reflects on why education is "an act of liberation and love", an act that sits in a state of perpetual but not uncomfortable tension with other more functional or transmission-related purposes. Stephen's views are clear, but his voice – even when incisively critical – is always respectful and fully grounded in experience.

Carly Waterman, principal, Lodge Park Academy, Northamptonshire

Educating with Purpose is not just timely, it's tremendous. Just when we are looking for a sense of direction, Stephen provides us with a complete vision for the future of our education system. Here, one of the most respected educators in the country re-examines the purpose of education and looks beyond the short-termism that has plagued our school system for far too long. This book is a coherent rallying cry for everyone who is determined to do the very best for our most dispossessed; for those of us who, as Stephen says, "will no longer accept a life well lived for the few" but demand it for all.

John Tomsett, headteacher

This book – and the maturity of thinking that lies within and behind it – shows the rich depth of Stephen's passion and integrity. It explores both place and purpose for us all, but specifically for education and educators. Within each page lies a depth of knowledge, research and experience applied through a lens of moral purpose. Stephen gives space to voices across different time periods, sectors and philosophical persuasions, yet all are aligned to a compelling conviction that creates undeniable agency and purpose.

Caroline Barlow, headteacher, Heathfield Community College, East Sussex

The timing of this book couldn't be more perfect. Within the context of the Covid-19 pandemic, the death of George Floyd in the US and the growth of the #BlackLivesMatter movement, all of which shine a light on our broken society, we in education have an opportunity to renew focus on what matters. Stephen's book is an easy-to-read, warts-and-all summary of the current position in education, including how we got into some of this mess. Now is the time to revisit philosophies to re-purpose the curriculum and realign aspects of education, so that we have the right drivers in place for school improvement.

Raj Unsworth, parent, chair of governors, trustee and governance geek

Stephen has produced an excellent book written during the international crisis caused by Covid-19. Framing his personal experience of leadership at headship and CEO-level against some of the works of the leading educational thinkers of the past and present day, Stephen's book sets the tone for us, during the pause created by Covid-19, to consider how education in schools may unfold over the next 10 years, with the next generation of leaders at the helm.

Jon Chaloner, vice-chair of Headteachers' Roundtable and CEO of GLF Schools

Perhaps the greatest curse of the English school system in recent years is an accountability system that has been set up in a way that has forced school leaders to think "I" not "we", "me" not "us". We have been encouraged to compete, to judge the performance of our schools only by comparing to others, to care about our own young people but not about the young people in the school down the road. While some still claim this drives standards up, more and more school leaders recognise the damage this has done and the toxicity it has created. This is a book for the rapidly growing movement of people who say, "No more." Stephen, one of the most credible and decent leaders we have, moves beyond the curriculum as a political battleground and brings an honesty that recognises complexity, nuance and all the grey areas that schools and people are made up of. How refreshing it is to read something that explodes the myth that a school curriculum can have breadth and depth in equal measure!

Jonny Uttley, CEO, The Education Alliance

As always, Stephen manages to combine deep and intellectually rigorous thinking with the straightforward, practical advice that arises from it. This book will not only make you think deeply but also help you plan your work more purposefully and effectively.

Professor Sam Twiselton OBE, director, Sheffield Institute of Education

I was one of the vulnerable students that *Educating with Purpose* champions and, take it from me, you should read this book. Stephen focuses on what matters and for whom. Every student matters and how this can be accomplished is discussed in an erudite and compassionate way. The book's focus is on empowering students, teachers and leaders and so re-purposing schools. Stephen's call to schools is to empower students to create a better and happier world. Our future, and theirs, needs this.

Vivienne Porritt, leadership consultant, strategic leader of #WomenEd and vice-president of the Chartered College of Teaching

Educating with Purpose is a thoughtful, challenging book that tackles the vital question: what is the purpose of education? Stephen's passion for working with disadvantaged children and young people shines throughout the book. It is a guide for every young teacher in determining their philosophy of education and provides practical guidance in important areas such as curriculum design. The book is written at an interesting time for education – the time is right for all teachers, educationalists, policymakers and stakeholders to have a national discussion on the purpose of education. *Educating with Purpose* is the ideal starting point for that discussion.

Sue Williamson, chief executive, SSAT

Stephen's intelligent and measured anger, matched by the acerbic wit of Stan Dupp's illustrations, shows that the battle for the heart of England's education system is not won, despite the ideological stranglehold it is in currently. The more young teachers and school leaders who are able to combine Stephen's wisdom with his keen eye for knowing a good idea from a false idol, the better when it comes to winning that battle.

Ian Gilbert, founder, Independent Thinking

Stephen has long been the "go to" person for moral, humane and realistic analysis of how our schools work and what we could do better, especially for the most disadvantaged pupils. This book is a deep and thought-provoking look at the purpose of education. It is vital reading for anyone who cares about the future of our young people and our society, which are too often disconnected in policymaking.

Fiona Millar, education writer and commentator

Stephen offers a book of hope against a backdrop of uncertainty for the education system. *Educating with Purpose* is a compendium of knowledge, practice and theory to support schools that seek to transform culture and to place developing people at the heart of school improvement. Having thrived for 30 years as a teacher and school leader in one of the most disadvantaged areas of the UK, Stephen offers valuable insight for policymakers who wish to evolve school policy based upon evidence, rather than ideology.

Ross Morrison McGill, CEO, Teacher Toolkit

What are our schools for? What do school leaders hope to achieve? This book offers deep debate and reflection that draws on a career of wide-ranging experience and study. Stephen pulls together the competing tensions that school leaders experience daily and helps the reader to consider the importance of maintaining alignment with vision. He considers leadership through the lens of impact upon young people and their communities, and helps to remind us what really matters.

Professor Dame Alison Peacock, CEO, Chartered College of Teaching

Educating with Purpose is a fantastic exploration into the heart and soul of education. Stephen skilfully, and with great care and insight, enables the reader to reflect and ponder their own educational purpose, linking theory and experience into a compelling narrative, proposing tools to reflect on your educational predispositions and enabling you to challenge your bias. Stephen concludes with a call to arms to re-purpose education for all the young people and communities we serve, driven by our values and heart. 2020 is just the beginning...

Nick Heard, executive director, National College of Education

This essential read of leadership practices curated and contextualised for educationalists is a refreshing, insightful and timely contribution to the discipline, given the global need to understand more about compassionate and purpose-driven leadership.

Professor Ben Laker, Henley Business School

A sharp analysis of the current educational landscape, a pop at some of our more bonkers practices, a theory of equity and justice for our most disadvantaged communities and, above all, a call for a more expansive vision for education. An important read.

Mary Myatt, education writer and speaker

Stephen skilfully explores different philosophies of education as he considers the fundamental issue of why we educate. His discussion draws on his extensive reading and careful reflection, and he offers a balance of theory and personal perspective based on his broad experience of education and leadership. He presents the compelling argument that we should all strive for "a life well lived" and do everything in our power to secure this for the young people in our care. The book is characterised by Stephen's typical honesty and frankness, his underpinning strong principles and commitment to social justice, together with, of course, a clear sense of purpose. It is peppered throughout with practical advice, grounded insights and sound wisdom.

Jill Berry, former headteacher, now leadership consultant

Stephen has managed to write a book about leadership that combines the latest research and data with decades of experience of being a leader in one of the most challenging environments in the country. He draws together reflections from fellow school leaders that will help you challenge your thinking, critique your perspective and help you answer "What's your purpose?" *Educating with Purpose* is a must-read for anyone thinking about moving into senior leadership and those of us already in it. However, it is also a book that we should buy for every person involved in making policy decisions about education. I feel energised for having read it.

Vic Goddard, author and co-principal of Passmores Academy, Essex

Stephen's latest book is packed full of knowledge, experience and real-life examples. From the early-career teacher to the experienced leader, you will finish this book after pausing many times to reflect on your own practice. It is invaluable to have an educator like Stephen who can write about leadership, wellbeing, the curriculum and more in a book that you won't want to finish!

Amjad Ali, founder, TryThisTeaching.com

Powerful, personal insights from a career working within some of the most disadvantaged communities in England create a compelling case for shifting educational debate from "what works" to "what matters". Now, more than ever before, a debate on the purpose of education is critical and, for that, this is essential reading.

Nick Brook, deputy general secretary, NAHT

This is a powerful book and a timely one. With a global pandemic shaking the foundations of the education system, many are looking to reconnect with the purpose of education and think afresh about the future. This is the perfect book to help on that journey. Stephen combines brilliantly an exploration of big ideas with the practical wisdom of an experienced headteacher. It is a book that reflects the qualities of its author: courage, insight, passion and integrity. It is a deeply personal book, both about motivation, the life of a headteacher and the different ways of making a real difference to the community around you.

Peter Hyman, co-director of Big Education and co-founder of School 21

For our children and grandchildren
From A-Z, Australia to Zachary
And all the people and places in between
That their education will enable them to have lives well lived

Thanks

First and foremost to Cath and the growing family – our children, their partners and a grandchild (soon to be grandchildren), who continue to enrich our lives in so many ways. To my mum and dad, sadly no longer with us, whose influence lives on.

To the staff, pupils, parents, directors and colleagues who have been part of my professional life and who wrote this story with me, in real time. Especially to Barry, Camilla, Liz and Paul, who trusted me to lead St Mary's and accompanied me on the ups and downs of the journey over 20 years. With thanks to Mike Humphries, who appointed me as a probationary teacher, supported and challenged me as a school improvement partner and advised me as a director. He was there throughout my career. To Anthony McNamara, Mike Webster and Father Luiz: coaches, mentors, confidantes and friends.

To Binks Neate-Evans, Sabrina Hobbs, Nav Sanghara, Ros McMullen and Dave Whitaker, all fellow members of Headteachers' Roundtable, who share their experiences and perspectives in this book.

To the brilliant Stan Dupp, whose illustrations have brought the book alive; a thousand words in each powerful image. Thanks also to Ian Gilbert, Sue Williamson, Ros McMullen and Professor Sam Twistelton, whose gentle but insightful critiques of an early draft of *Educating with Purpose* helped me to write this book. Also, thanks to Julia Moore, Jon Chaloner and Malcolm Laverty (aka the illustrious Stan Dupp), who edited drafts or made suggestions to improve the text, or both.

And finally to Alex at John Catt for giving me this opportunity to publish *Educating with Purpose*, Isla for editing it, and their team for ordering, organising and printing it.

Contents

Foreword

In 2015, the SSAT published a pamphlet for its Redesigning Schooling series, *A Vision for Education – beyond five-year policy cycles*, written by its Vision 2040 group. Having been involved in the group's early stages, I was asked to write the foreword. This is how it began:

> *"How does that old joke go?*
> *'Sir, can you tell me the way to the city centre?' 'Well, if I was you, I wouldn't start from here!'*
> *Obviously, we are where we are. We have an educational system that has many strengths with scattered pockets of excellence, driven by a workforce rich with talented, committed individuals. And yet, we're frustrated. There's a strong sense that our education system could be so much better than it is. Too many young people are short-changed; the inequity in the system is vast and, given the resources at our disposal, most people would recognise that where we are is not where we should be. But we are where we are. The first question is – where do we want to get to?"*

The Vision 2040 group was led by Stephen Tierney. Much of that paper resonates strongly, five years on. But, actually, I think I was wrong about "the first question". Having read *Educating with Purpose*, I'm certain that we need to start with that much deeper question: what is education for? Before we rush to planning the mechanics of a journey to some imagined destination, we need to consider the fundamentals: our motivation, purposes, values – the reason for doing any of it. Otherwise we'll find ourselves off course as soon as we start.

For many years, Stephen has been, for me, something of a touchstone for moral purpose in our system. In his work as a school leader and system leader, as well as in his writing, he communicates an earnest, passionate determination to confront the barriers that impede leaders and teachers serving disadvantaged communities. The notion of service permeates everything he says and does. *Educating with Purpose* is a superb exploration of the conflicting, competing pressures school leaders face every day, forcing us to reconsider the fundamentals. What's it all for? What matters? Even when we think we've got a strong sense of our purpose, weighing up our positions along the various axes, how do we enact that purpose? This is easier said than done. Stephen's trademark is matching pragmatism to his idealism, and he skilfully maps out a case for pausing to re-examine and re-purpose numerous areas of policy at both school and system level.

As Stephen references, a perfect example of these considerations is the imperative to develop a deeper anti-racist philosophy in schools. It's uncontroversial that placing anti-racism at the heart of our educational purpose requires a strong element of personal empowerment and preparation for citizenship. However, the cultural transmission element is likely to need much closer self-examination. Have we been transmitting an absolutely explicit anti-racist message through our curriculum? Have our students been taught the breadth and depth of knowledge they need to fully understand why, in 2020, Black Lives Matter needs to exist as a call to action? It's hard to think of knowledge much more powerful. How is black history explored beyond the story of empire, slavery and the US civil rights movement? Where are the positive narratives that reframe perceptions and change attitudes? What would it be like to be a BAME student in your school engaging in your curriculum? This is where educating with purpose comes in. It's not easy but, as Stephen sums up so beautifully, "we must sing into existence this future". That's the duty of all educators – to do the work and make the change.

Tom Sherrington, author and education consultant

CHAPTER 1
Why we educate

My first book, *Liminal Leadership* (2016), started with a story about a priest and a taxi driver who died and were met by St Peter at the pearly gates. The punchline is that the taxi driver got straight into heaven, because people prayed when he drove, whereas the priest had to wait a couple of years in Purgatory, because people slept when he preached. It's a story about purpose. It's also a story about how purpose can too easily become narrowed when we focus on a singular aspect or a particular measure.

In the decade past, there was an increased focus on the development of a knowledge-rich curriculum built around subject classifications. Schools were required to give greater priority to the intellectual development of children and young people. The national curriculum, examination syllabi and accountability metrics were all used to support this. Latterly, Ofsted became involved, with its focus on the curriculum as the substance of education and its adoption of a particular definition of learning: " … an alteration in long-term memory. If nothing has altered in long-term memory, nothing has been learned" (Ofsted, 2019). This is in keeping with a purpose of education rooted in an aspect of cultural transmission and the influence of cognitive science.

During the past decade, there has also been a wider movement within English education to be more evidence-informed. Organisations like the Education Endowment Foundation have supported research in education and published a range of guidance documents. These usefully summarise the research evidence as currently known. ResearchED, a grassroots organisation, hosts tens of thousands of teachers every year at very low-cost Saturday conferences, providing an opportunity to listen to a number of speakers providing insights into aspects of research evidence. ResearchED is now a worldwide movement.

These changes went to the heart of what matters; they significantly influenced the purpose of education. The equilibrium point has been reset. A greater focus on the intellectual means less time for other aspects of education. This matters because education is a "teleological practice" (Biesta, 2015). *Telos* in Greek literally means "end" – an ultimate aim or the purpose of a practice. Purpose provides a sense of direction: it is a pole star that may act as a guiding light as we travel towards it and an end point from which we may look back at the journey. Without purpose, education becomes merely transactional rather than potentially transformative.

As I write this on the eve of what would have been my mum's 80th birthday, I'm taken back to her eulogy. It ended with a thanks to family and friends for helping her to have "a life well lived". This phrase provides a powerful telos. It doesn't seek to detail the whole of the educational endeavour; rather, it becomes a useful pole star to guide us. As teachers and school leaders, our aim is to help all children and young people to have a life well lived. This requires the equilibrium point to be reset again. A life well lived doesn't exclude the development of the intellectual; in fact, it embraces it, but sets it within a greater purpose. A purpose in which different elements of a balanced education – moral, spiritual, aesthetic, creative, emotional and physical – are held in tension. This different "why" has consequences. It impacts on the "what" and the "how".

When we get education right, the impact can be life-long and life-changing. The story of the plain-speaking Yorkshireman emphasises this. When meeting his children's headteacher (the children by now in their thirties and forties), he responded to a question about whether the school had provided them with a good education by stating, "It's too early to tell." Education is holistic and long-term. Schooling is a crucial early phase of it.

Schooling, a uniquely human concept and construct, is not the totality of a person's education. We need a purpose that encapsulates both schooling *and* education. My mum's schooling in a post-war Birmingham secondary modern was less valuable than it could have been. My dad missed a whole year of junior school owing to rheumatic fever. However, my parents valued education and attained degrees when middle-aged. They both worked in education, as a teacher in a special school in Liverpool and a lecturer in further education respectively. To justify the time and the expense, schooling must be of value to the person and to society. It must have a purpose powerful enough to justify its continuation.

In a life well lived, education is a holistic act of love. Started by parents, it involves different communities over time and is subject to personal intent. It is a means of helping people to earn a living, contribute positively to society and find a *reason* for living. It exemplifies one of the great tensions. Education and schooling have to wrestle with how we meet the needs of both the "I" and the "we". A life well lived requires a giving of our best to each and every person, developing and forming them in a community, while allowing them to grow and flourish as unique individuals.

In *Liminal Leadership*, I quote Desmond Tutu writing about the word *ubuntu*, which may be translated as "a person is a person through other people" or "I am because we are". We become fully human through our relationships with other people. When education and learning are viewed from a purely individualistic perspective, this fails to grasp the importance of the "we". The role education can play in the formation of relationships, communities and a cohesive society may be lost. But if education lacks a focus on the individual, the importance of the "I" is lost. The dangers of imposing someone else's agenda or biases are all too present, but there is also the absence of discovering who we are and what we might be. We may never develop the sense of self that is a critical part of determining and having control over our future.

Frank Coffield, emeritus professor of education at the UCL Institute of Education, has expressed his concern at Ofsted's adopted definition of learning, describing it as "not fit for purpose". His concerns were that the definition was "one-dimensional, individualistic and, though it may be appropriate for psychological laboratory experiments, it is not appropriate for education". Coffield suggested a more expansive and arguably more appropriate definition of learning with respect to education. By focusing on what we mean by learning, we can often discern underlying purpose.

"Learning refers to significant enhancements in knowledge, capabilities, values, attitudes or understanding (including but going beyond the acquisition of factual knowledge) by individuals, groups, organisations or society."   Coffield (2019)

Coffield's definition explicitly identifies capabilities, values and attitudes alongside knowledge and understanding, further expanding learning to encompass groups, organisations or society. This is significant in that it creates a challenge to our assessment of outcomes. These are currently individualistic and orientated towards learning that can be assessed through written examinations. Coffield's definition raises the question of whether we are simply valuing what we measure, as opposed to expanding what we measure to align with what we value.

Our education system is relatively good at assessing intellectual outcomes, particularly with respect to subject knowledge. Looking at school performance tables, for English schools, the intellectual predominates. GCSEs are orientated towards certain disciplines, and certain subjects within disciplines, with the arts and technology marginalised. There is little to recognise other important aspects of education.

The assessment of schools suffers from what could be termed "construct under-representation". This is concerned with the assessment being too small. There are elements missing from the assessment that should have been included to draw valid inferences about the construct. This not only undermines the validity of the conclusions we wish to draw about how effective a school is at educating children and young people, but it also undermines more holistic views about the purpose of education. Things that matter are no longer considered important simply because they are not measured.

Gert Biesta supports a wider definition of learning, expressing concerns about the narrow view being taken in many of what Pasi Sahlberg calls the "Global Educational Reform Movements". Biesta highlights the difference between a good education as opposed to an effective one; the linkage between purpose and learning is of paramount importance.

> "... the point of education is that students learn something, that they learn it for a reason, and that they learn it from someone ... education always needs to engage with questions of content, purpose and relationships."   Biesta (2015)

He proposes three interrelating domains encapsulating the purpose of education: qualification (transmission and acquisition of knowledge, skills and dispositions), socialisation (initiation of children and young people in traditions – cultural, professional, political, religious – and ways of being and doing) and subjectification (positive or negative impact on the pupil as a person; the way in which children and young people come to exist as subjects of initiative and responsibility rather than as objects of the actions of others).

Balancing these different domains is crucial when educating in the most disadvantaged communities, where schools need to provide enhanced levels of support to children and young people. Negative experiences of schooling can leave families trapped, with limited belief in their own ability to control their lives and low or no confidence in schools to change the narrative. The lack of subjectification (being director of one's own destiny) can lead to disengagement with schooling. Qualifications and the learning within them are perceived as an irrelevance and unachievable, rather than a passport to a better future. Having been pushed to the edge of society or beyond, the outsider sees little value in maintaining traditions that don't value them in return. It is only in melding a multidimensional educational purpose, working with the local community and other agencies, that we can bring about change over time.

The skilled teacher aligns their pedagogical knowledge with the context of the classroom and different aspects of education (content, purpose and relationships) in order to help pupils learn and become better learners. Biesta (2015), referencing the work of John Hattie (2009), exemplifies this using the relatively poor evidence for the impact of homework/home learning on pupil attainment. It is worth noting that there is quite a difference between studies for primary and secondary-aged children, with the impact on the latter significantly higher. In the qualification domain, it would be easy to dismiss home learning as a waste of time for primary-aged pupils. However, requiring a pupil to take responsibility for their own learning "outside of the controlling 'gaze' of the teacher" (Biesta, 2015) would impact positively within the subjectification domain. The pupil would acquire a greater sense of ownership of their learning. During the Covid-19 lockdown in the UK in spring 2020, those pupils who had a greater sense of themselves as subjects (those who know and can act) were better equipped to enhance their acquisition of knowledge in the months of partial school closure.

Biesta's point is that just identifying what works is simplistic and at times unhelpful. Considering what works "in relation to a particular purpose" allows us to answer the bigger question: what matters? Focusing too narrowly on one domain can lead to distress within another. The past decade brought relatively modest improvements in some academic measures in England, but a significant downturn in pupils' attitudes towards their lives compared with young people in other countries. In terms of life satisfaction, our 15-year-olds were ranked 69th out of the 72 countries that participated in PISA 2018 (OECD, 2019). Headlines appeared about how unhappy our young people were and are. Many think there now needs to be a rebalancing of schools' purpose. Schools are for learning. But definitions of learning expose clear fault lines in the different purposes of education.

Definitions of learning aren't created within a vacuum. They are shaped by what we consider the purpose of education to be, the context in which we work and what we value most. Those choices are manifested in how and what is taught. The extent to which this view is informed and coherent varies. At times, too little thought has been given to alternative thinking or views. Part of making an informed decision is acquiring a sound knowledge of competing philosophies of education and then melding these into a unifying purpose of education, set within a context and ethical framework. This may be guided centrally, but needs to be brought alive by informed school leaders, teachers and communities at a local level. The differences between national cohesion versus the local context, the uniqueness of different phases of education/schools versus sharing best practice and focusing on the continuity of pupils' learning, and the different types of schools and alternative provision all contribute to the purpose of education as it is enacted.

An understanding of purpose allows you to critique. For example, I believe the Early Career Framework (ECF) for new teachers is a major step forward in England. Supporting young teachers with additional non-contact time, an experienced coach and a curriculum of further professional studies will be one element needed to retain a greater number of people within the profession. The inclusion of cognitive load theory, as an underpinning theory, within the ECF is eminently sensible. However, the omission of attachment theory is not. This is a purpose issue. I believe that schools must balance the emotional wellbeing and mental health of children and young people with their intellectual development. If you like, schools have a significant part to play in making kids cleverer, happier, confident and moral. I would also add safer.

If the past decade focused on what works, the decade ahead must focus on what matters. The purpose of education must move to the heart of the educational debate. It is central, not an add-on. Purpose is the associate and precursor of effectiveness – what works. It will significantly influence what we do next.

CHAPTER 2
Four philosophies of education

Imagine that Greta Thunberg, the young Swedish climate change activist, organised one of her Friday "strikes" in your school's locality. Half the pupils went to listen to her speak and march for climate change; half stayed in school and attended their normal Friday afternoon lessons. Which of your pupils would you feel more proud of? Which would you consider to have really taken to heart the central message of the education you are providing? Would you admonish those pupils who went on the march, or those who attended their normal lessons? Or would you do nothing, in essence accepting or condoning the personal choice of each?

When speaking to groups of school leaders, I often use this question to help them expose and explore what they believe the purpose of education to be. Or, more precisely, which of the various philosophies of education they think should be given priority. When making decisions, we have to get off the

They've had a makeover: empowerment; transmission; employment and citizenship!

fence and act. It is a way of exposing the tensions around educational purpose and a way of ensuring we are comfortable with the aspects given a greater and lesser importance.

Dylan Wiliam (2013) identifies four philosophies that underpin the purpose of education: personal empowerment, cultural transmission, preparation for work and preparation for citizenship. I would summarise the aim of each of these as:

1. To develop the potential of the child (personal empowerment). A balance is needed between the acquisition of skills and knowledge, both of which need to be applied. In *Pedagogy of the Oppressed*, Paulo Freire reminds us that "a person learns to swim in the water, not in a library", hence his focus on praxis (thought and action). Underpinning this is the desire to "allow young people to take greater control of their own lives" (Wiliam, 2013).
2. To pass on "the best which has been thought and said" (cultural transmission). The focus is almost exclusively on knowledge acquisition and the development of the intellect. E.D. Hirsch Jr (1988) develops a key element with his work on cultural literacy – an anthropological view of education involving "the transmission to children of the specific information shared by the adults of the group". This is developed using Michael Young's idea of "powerful knowledge" (2014), which is more appropriate when considering specialised knowledge.
3. To prepare young people for life and work (preparation for work). The focus is on problem solving and real-world experiences. As more educated workers are more productive, there is a correlation between educational achievement and economic prosperity.
4. To build communities and overcome social disadvantage (preparation for citizenship). This focuses on the school's context and seeks to support the development of social capital within families and the local community. Key to its success is ensuring young people are sufficiently well informed about substantive and current issues to make decisions and take action in support of the democratic process.

All these philosophies have impacted, to a greater or lesser extent, on my views and the decisions I took as a teacher and school leader. Personal empowerment and cultural transmission have a theoretical base that I will explore in more detail in the chapters ahead. So much of my experience in schools involved serving disadvantaged communities in the North West of England, and I soon realised that I could not assume young people would come to school with a broad, rich set of experiences. If we were to develop their potential to the fullest, the school would need to help compensate for what they had missed as part of family life. There was also a need to ensure that they did not take a fatalistic view of life.

Personal empowerment, the ability to take greater control of your life, is covered extensively in the work and writings of Freire (1921-97). He believed the main purpose of education was to give people greater control of their own lives, developing them to their full potential. Defining his own telos for education as "No longer part of the mass, but one of the people", Freire believed education must enable people to make a deliberate, informed decision to participate in the political, social and cultural transformation of their community, region or country.

Having initially studied law, Freire became involved in the education of poor, illiterate adults in Brazil. In the introduction to his book *Pedagogy of the Oppressed* (first translated into English in 1970, but I quote a 2017 edition), written while he was in exile after the 1964 military coup in Brazil, he stated:

> *"Accordingly, this admittedly tentative work is for radicals. I am certain that Christians and Marxists, though they may disagree with me in part or whole, will continue reading to the end. But the reader who dogmatically assumes closed, 'irrational' positions will reject the dialogue I hope this book will open."*
>
> Freire (2017)

His belief that Christians would read to the end may have been influenced by his Catholic upbringing and the impact of South American liberation theology on his thinking and writing. Liberation theology places a great emphasis on addressing poverty and social injustices, as well as more spiritual matters.

My dad was a member of the St Vincent de Paul Society, a worldwide organisation that seeks to tackle poverty at a local level. The Vincentians can often be spotted holding a collection box outside church, at the end of Mass. Dad, as the treasurer of the local society, was often called on to help those in greatest need. By the end of my teenage years, I was his chauffeur, food box carrier and furniture mover. Over the decades, Dad quietly and privately helped out numerous people. It was a faith lived out through practice. Service to the poor was a matter of justice, not charity. The foundations of who we become, as so often, were laid out in my early experiences.

Freire's call to service was referenced in his writings. These are often linked to scripture:

"From these pages I hope at least the following will endure: my trust in the people, and my faith in men and women, and in the creation of a world in which it is easier to love." Freire (2017)

The references to "love" and "faith" resonate with 1 Corinthians 13:13: "And now these three remain: faith, hope and love. But the greatest of these is love." And Freire's focus on the need for people to become "fully human" may be found in John 10:10: "I have come that they may have life, and have it to the full." Freire viewed education from a broader perspective of people's emerging understanding of their history as individuals and as mankind: a people who have been, who are and who will be; a culture that has been, that is and that will be. He believed in the potential for people to influence and impact upon the world and their place within it. Life is not a preordained destiny. We can set our own direction. In viewing how people face various challenges, he notes they "are not limited to a single reaction pattern. They organize themselves, choose the best response, test themselves, act, and change in the very act of responding. They do all this consciously, as one uses a tool to deal with a problem." This is the empowerment Freire sought to engender.

Fundamental to this is the belief that people and the world in which they live are intrinsically linked, as opposed to the world and people existing as separate, discrete entities. In creating and re-creating the world and their relationship with it, "[people] add to it something of their own making ... by creating culture". Freire sees a dynamic reality that is open to influence and change. Authentic learning is applied, not solely theoretical; education is praxis. This is an important aspect of working with disadvantaged communities. Their often limited experience of controlling their own lives can be disempowering. Telling them they can influence the direction of their lives is not as powerful as their directly experiencing it.

Although personal empowerment is of significant importance, Freire's work with illiterate people doesn't transfer directly into the subject-based curriculum. As a secondary science teacher, I knew there was a body of scientific knowledge and disciplinary way of working that students had to know, understand and be able to apply. It wasn't always, or often, associated with individual problems, experiences or the social context in which they lived.

There is, however, an importance and beauty in understanding the structures and behaviour of our natural and physical world. This knowledge forms part of an examination system. Success in examinations provides passports to further study, employment and enhanced life opportunities. This substantive and disciplinary knowledge is one aspect of the philosophy of education termed cultural transmission.

Cultural transmission is often encapsulated in the phrase "the best which has been thought and said in the world". This is from Matthew Arnold's 1869 essay *Culture and Anarchy*. His essay was written at a time of significant social upheaval: the Industrial Revolution in Britain had led to substantial and permanent changes to where people lived and how they earned their living. Arnold viewed culture as a way of addressing this increasingly fractured society, in order to create greater social cohesion and unity.

The dangers of failing to do this were becoming all too apparent. The increasing demands of the working class for political representation led to the Hyde Park Railings Affair in 1866. This was an example of the "anarchy" in the title of Arnold's paper.

> " ... *a large crowd gathered at Hyde Park in London to hear speakers on voting rights. They were confronted by police when the government declared the meeting an illegal assembly. Soldiers were called out when 200,000 people entered the park anyway, knocking down fences meant to keep them out.*"
> Logan (2012)

Before Arnold's *Culture and Anarchy* essay, culture had generally been associated with an individual's knowledge of various subjects – for example, Greek and Latin – or their appreciation of the arts. But Arnold's view was clear: culture was *not* associated with a body of knowledge linked to high culture and possessed by individuals primarily within the socially elite, thus setting them apart. Arnold's original work is often misinterpreted.

He redefined culture from a purely personal to a societal perspective. Individuals within society were required to use their knowledge to leave the world a "better and happier place". Culture must have a strong dimension of social justice and lead to greater equality. This was to be achieved using knowledge, in "fresh and free thought", to challenge the status quo as part of an ongoing process of evaluation.

Rooted in Arnold's view that "the best which has been thought and said" is not a particular work or set of works but is instead a process of critique, Martin Robinson (2018) proposes that a good curriculum invites pupils into a conversation with the "extended community of minds that stretches back into the past and will stretch beyond us into the future". Rather than referring to a "knowledge-rich" curriculum, Robinson sees a rich curriculum as one that "tells stories that enable us to see more clearly, more thoughtfully and more wisely from a wide range of perspectives".

One particular aspect of cultural transmission is cultural literacy (Hirsch, 1988), the means by which a nation's citizens may communicate effectively with each other. Cultural literacy is built on a shared knowledge and understanding of key vocabulary, ideas and events that form part of a nation's ongoing language. This brings clearly into focus "whose" culture should take precedence within education. The imposition of the cultural norms and perception of history of a more powerful group on those who are less powerful or oppressed embeds injustice within a system. Alongside cultural literacy is the increasingly important impact of disciplines, represented as subjects, on a school's curriculum.

This book hopes to explore critical questions relating to purpose and its enactment within the curriculum. The various educational philosophies sit within a greater perspective of the purpose of education and what we consider a well-educated person to be. Developing the intellect is one obvious outcome of schooling. However, the warning of a Boston headteacher who had experienced the horrors of the concentration camps in World War II suggests it is not enough. She had witnessed knowledgeable people commit unspeakable atrocities. Hence her belief that "reading, writing and arithmetic are important only if they serve to make our children more human".

People are the real substance of education and it is to the purpose of bringing them fully alive, enabling them to have lives well lived and ensuring the same for others, that we must turn our attention.

CHAPTER 3
Personal empowerment

As I wrote earlier, a balance is needed between the acquisition of skills and knowledge, both of which need to be applied, and underpinning this is the desire to "allow young people to take greater control of their own lives" (Wiliam, 2013).

A person's opportunity to reflect – to think deeply and critically about an issue – and their ability to act without unnecessary limitations determine their quantum of empowerment. The extent to which a person is a subject (those who know and act) as opposed to an object (those who are known and acted upon) is intrinsically linked to whether they are liberated or oppressed and to what degree. The challenge is to transform the world into one in which we may all become fully human and more humane.

Personal empowerment, though a necessary first step, isn't the end goal. Rather, personal empowerment should be used to help develop and raise up a whole community. Its telos is greater social justice. Education should lead to social, political, economic and cultural transformation through empowered individuals. Education must be an act of liberation, enabling people to become free from unnecessary external constraints or limiting internal ones.

The decade in which I was born, the 1960s, was one of oppression: women, people from BAME backgrounds, people with disabilities and the LGBTQ+ community experienced prejudicial and unequal treatment. At the start of that decade there was literally no protection in law to prevent discrimination in its various forms. In fact, the reverse was true. It was perfectly legal to discriminate based on gender, race, disability or sexuality. Education has been part of the process of change over the past six decades and now equality is enshrined in statute, if not always reality. These challenges continue in these and other areas of inequality and there is a lack of equity to address particularly for those who are socioeconomically disadvantaged – a characteristic for which there is no protection in law.

The extent to which we humanise or dehumanise depends on the interaction, relationship and power dynamic between people. Freire expresses this interaction in terms of an oppressor/oppressed relationship. The oppressors, a ruling elite, superimpose their reality and their culture on people in order to preserve the current social order – an order through which the elite disproportionately benefit. There are many parallels between Freire's observations in Brazil, more than half a century ago, and what we can observe in England in 2020, where the differences between the affluent/advantaged and those who are disadvantaged or marginalised are stark.

> *"The pursuit of full humanity, however, cannot be carried out in isolation or individualism, but only in fellowship and solidarity; therefore it cannot unfold in the antagonistic relationships between oppressors and oppressed. No one can be authentically human while he prevents others from being so."*   Freire (2017)

One of the fundamentals of this relationship is the ability of the oppressor to prescribe or impose a choice, their choice, on the oppressed. The oppressed must conform, consequently becoming trapped in their belief about their own unworthiness and fatalistic about their lack of life control. As a school leader, teacher or parent, you are faced with this challenge. When is it acceptable to impose and implement on others for either their own good or the greater good of the family or community? Is it right to impose performance-related pay on teachers or insist that every 15 and 16-year-old studies either history or geography? Can these be justified in every situation, some situations or not at all? Are they acts of beneficence and justice or the unnecessary acts of the powerful?

Education, as an act of liberation and love, should enable and support both the oppressor and the oppressed in resetting the social order. Both are dehumanised by the power imbalance within the relationship. Paradoxically, in the early individualistic stages of liberation, Freire witnessed the people promoted to overseer or another position of responsibility/authority becoming oppressors themselves – "more of a tyrant than the owner himself". Freire maintains that it is only the oppressed who can truly liberate both themselves and their oppressor. Disadvantaged communities – the families and individuals living within them – need to be empowered as part of the process of ensuring greater social justice.

To achieve this personal empowerment and ultimately social transformation, Freire proposes that education must be about posing problems – a process of "acts of cognition, not transferrals of information" that "affirms men and women as beings in the process of *becoming* – as unfinished, uncompleted beings in and with a likewise unfinished reality". Challenges and aspirations – in a place, at a given time – will consist of a series of "ideas, concepts, hopes, doubts, values and challenges". When considered together, they constitute what Freire termed a generative theme.

Climate control, equality and equity form some of the key generative themes of our times. A series of complex problems can be debated in each of these themes. Ultimately these debates must lead to action.

For example, in climate control, there are a range of issues that could be discussed. Could climate change be most effectively addressed by reducing the world's population, by having fewer children? By changing our diets and decreasing our meat and dairy intake? By eating more locally produced food; changing our farming methods; protecting the rainforests and planting more trees; reducing consumerism and materialism; reusing rather than recycling or throwing away products; reducing our use of energy and increasing our reliance on renewables; changing transportation systems to increase public transport; reducing the use of cars; or changing our working habits?

Likewise, when considering equality and discrimination, many questions could be asked. Equality is now enshrined in statute, but what is the reality of people's lived experiences? To what extent is corrosive and persistent low-level discrimination an issue? What are the major issues still being experienced? What laws are still not being properly enacted? Can the gender pay gap be reduced without greater social change with respect to parenting? Why is economic disadvantage (poverty) not included in the list of protected characteristics? Should discrimination based upon socioeconomic status be illegal? What should happen when groups with protected characteristics have opposing views? Is there a hierarchy of protected characteristics?

To what extent are global migration patterns being driven by a lack of global equity (huge differences in living standards and quality of life between the richest and poorest countries)? Can we welcome to the UK everyone who wishes to come here? If not, what is the limit and who should be allowed to enter and who should be refused? Are there "good immigrants" (highly qualified; possessing the right skills) and "bad immigrants" (poor qualifications; low-skilled)? How does this fit with your view of humanity?

And to what extent should these themes form key aspects within a school's curriculum? In a later chapter, on curriculum principles, I'll explain two key principles of this more thematic problem-posing approach to education, namely relevance and coherence. They have significant implications for the organisation of a school's curriculum.

The 'banking' concept of education

Freire's critique of the education system is encapsulated in his idea of education as a process of "banking". In the banking concept of education, teachers are the subjects, with pupils seen as the objects. Pupils as passive recipients become "lifeless and petrified" – for example, through a curriculum that is imposed upon them and has limited, if any, connection to their own experiences. Such a curriculum is presented as a static, compartmentalised body of knowledge that is filed away but not acted on. Freire says it is education as an "act of depositing", with the choice of what and how to deposit determined apart from the pupils.

> *"Our traditional curriculum, disconnected from life, centred on words emptied of the reality they are meant to represent, lacking in concrete activity ... "*   Freire (1974)

According to Freire, knowledge becomes a gift "bestowed by those who consider themselves knowledgeable upon those whom they consider to know nothing". It is a stark statement. He asks: in reality, is anyone an "utter ignoramus or perfect sage?"

For Freire, this is a part of the oppressor/oppressed relationship. It is an anti-dialogical approach constituting cultural invasion, a key instrument used in oppression. Any large collection of top-down determined content – in present-day education through national standards, curricula and examination syllabi – constitutes the imposing of the world view of one group on to another. This is exacerbated by an education solely focused on transmission and the development of the intellect, in the absence of a social, political and economic critique. People of different genders, races, ethnicities and sexualities, people of faith and those with disabilities or of different socioeconomic classes have all been subject to this "cultural invasion".

"One of the basic elements of the relationship between oppressor and oppressed is prescription. Every prescription represents the imposition of one individual's choice upon another, transforming the consciousness of the person prescribed to into one that conforms with the prescriber's consciousness."   Freire (2017)

In contrast to this, Freire is consistent in his view that education "must be formed with, not for, the oppressed (whether individuals or peoples) in the incessant struggle to regain their humanity". This includes content, pedagogy and the outcomes in terms of policies, programmes or projects upon which actions are based. Freire offers the following critique of the banking concept of education, exposing the contradictions in the teacher-student relationship:

" ... banking education maintains and even stimulates the contradiction through the following attitudes and practices, which mirror oppressive society as a whole:

a.   the teacher teaches and the students are taught;
b.   the teacher knows everything and the student knows nothing;
c.   the teacher thinks and the students are thought about;
d.   the teacher talks and the students listen – meekly;
e.   the teacher disciplines and the students are disciplined;
f.   the teacher chooses and enforces his choice, and the students comply;
g.   the teacher acts and the students have the illusion of acting through the action of the teacher;

h. the teacher chooses the program content, and the students (who were not consulted) adapt to it;

i. the teacher confuses the authority of knowledge with his or her own professional authority, which she or he sets in opposition to the freedom of the students;

j. the teacher is the Subject of the learning process, while the pupils are mere objects."

Freire (2017)

Freire saw these anti-dialogical actions as a "conquest"; an imposition by a conqueror on the conquered. This conquest is supported in three ways: divide and rule, manipulation and cultural invasion. It is possible to see parallels and the application of a number of the tools within our current education system.

We stratify schools (through system-level accountability), teachers (through school-level accountability and performance pay) and pupils (through examination grades). Freire would view the use of zero-tolerance behaviour systems, "flattening the grass" and the exclusion or moving on of some of our most vulnerable children and young people as dehumanising. They are all part of an oppressive system.

In a 2019 article for *Tes* (tinyurl.com/ybgjm6mw), I wrote about the power dynamic within the current accountability system, applying Freire's thinking to Ofsted and its new inspection framework for England. I cast Ofsted in the role of the oppressor and exposed the impact of the accountability system on school leaders, who have become the system's overseers. Here is an extract:

OFSTED MIGHT HAVE A NEW FRAMEWORK, BUT THE SAME OLD PROBLEMS REMAIN
If Ofsted really wants to work with schools, it needs to rebalance the power dynamic and ditch the grading system once and for all …

… True dialogue needs an appropriate power dynamic – in the absence of that, it easily becomes a monologue or an interrogation. When a headteacher gets the long-feared call, the current power dynamic means that we are not all in this together – we are all in this very differently. As a school leader, you know that your organisation will, after a visit that is little more than cursory, in the totality of the work done over many years, be summed up in a high-stakes, cliff-edged, one-word judgement. 'Outstanding' leads to freedoms, opportunities and access to more funding. 'Inadequate' leads to ignominy, loss of staff critical to the work and future success of the school, falling pupil numbers and financial difficulty.

There was and still is the potential to change this. Ofsted and politicians need to step up and work with the profession. The power dynamic needs to be rebalanced. Freire would call for the oppressor and the oppressed to be released from their bonds and focus on addressing the problem of how to help improve the school.

Three simple suggestions come to mind: the removal of grading from the whole process; all evidence forms and evidence used by the inspection team to be provided, in real time and unredacted, to the school; and fundamental reform of Ofsted's complaints process.

Through the consultation, Headteachers' Roundtable proposed that the grading of individual sections of the framework be removed as a first step. Unfortunately, this has fallen on deaf ears – it would have been hugely symbolic and potentially revolutionary. The 'no grading' of sections of the report would have been a catalyst to remove the overall judgement grade. Dialogue is commensurate with narrative, not with grading, and is even more important in contentious and subjective areas such as curriculum.

By releasing all documents as they are written – the school should have joint and individual ownership – a real sense of partnership and agency would become palpable. Knowledge is power – so empower school leaders with the knowledge currently only available to the inspectors. These documents are likely to reveal the very real contradictions, variations and potential areas of focus that are part of any two-day visit to a school. The current clinical inspection report with all its certainties isn't real or believable: 'the school may want to consider further ... There seems some evidence to suggest ... Greater focus on x may be useful' are a much more real and arguably a more valid set of conclusions to reach, tentative as they should be.

Ofsted's complaints system is the final part of the rebalancing of power. It is currently so heavily weighted in favour of Ofsted that schools either don't bother, give up mid-process or are left frustrated with what they perceive as wrong judgements. Where a complaint is made, any report should remain unpublished until the complaint is resolved. Much better a delay than false or misleading information being publicly available. There is no need to publish reports quickly; most Ofsted reports are historical by a year or more. There must also be a wholly independent panel at the final stage of the process, at each stage of judgements, for as long as we have them, and commentary can be amended. People have to have confidence that grievances about reports will be listened to and will be seen to be listened to. They also need to believe they will be acted on.

Ofsted would possibly struggle with all of these changes. Its position of being all-powerful – I've always tended to think that was God's job – would be challenged. Professional dialogue with an expertly trained educator who is open to challenge, being challenged and having to engage in a two-way, informed and sometimes difficult conversation, would become just that.

CHAPTER 4
The organisation of education

Freire imagined a reconceptualisation of how education was organised, formed around a "culture circle" in "new institutions of popular culture". Content and pedagogy would be fundamentally rethought; the content of education, the content for dialogue, would be determined by the group itself.

Freire's philosophical approach, realised in his practice, was that the solutions to problems must be created *with* the people, never for them or imposed on them. Education must help to ensure that the people feel powerful – that is, they have the capacity for choice and they must be able to exercise that choice and "enter the historical process critically". Freire defines culture as "all human creation" and as such invites the whole of humanity into cultural formation, transmission and transformation.

> "… culture is just as much a clay doll made by artists who are his peers as it is the work of a great sculptor, a great painter, a great mystic, or a great philosopher; that culture is the poetry of lettered poets and also the poetry of his own popular songs …" Freire (1974)

There is neither high culture nor, by definition, low culture. There is simply culture which encompasses the whole. In seeking to promote personal empowerment, the content of education must be based on the participants' current concrete reality – the challenges they face and the aspirations they have, leading to an iterative reflection/action process in which their potential is fully realised and they become fully human. Integral to Freire's approach was the teacher as a coordinator of the learning.

> "The role of the problem-posing educator is to create, together with the students, the conditions under which knowledge at the level of the doxa is superseded by true knowledge, at the level of the logos." Freire (2017)

In a pupil-centred classroom, the teacher maintains a position of authority. This authority is used to support pupils to become increasingly self-directed and capable of producing their own knowledge. Through the formation and continued interrogation of the evidence, experiences and information available, the teacher and pupils continually reform their thinking. Some knowledge is provided by the teacher "just in time". This helps to move beliefs from those unrelated to reason or reality (doxa) to those based on reason and evidence (logos).

The importance of the teacher-pupil relationship cannot be understated. There must be no contradictions. Students are not objects; they must remain subjects within the educational process.

> *"The teacher is no longer merely the-one-who-teaches, but one who himself is taught in dialogue with the students, who in turn while being taught also teach. They become jointly responsible for a process in which all grow. In this process, arguments based on 'authority' are no longer valid; in order to function, authority must be on the side of freedom, not against it. Here, no one teaches another, nor is anyone self-taught."*
> Freire (2017)

Freire saw dialogue as an intrinsically human activity. As such, a dialogical approach was central to his vision of education and ultimately its transformative purpose. Dialogue as praxis (reflection and action) involved giving people an informed voice to talk about key issues for them and their community; to organise and unite around the issues and to bring about change.

> *"More often than not, we have attempted to transfer the knowledge to the people verbally, as if we could give lessons in democracy while regarding popular participation in the exercise of power as 'absurd and immoral'. We lacked – and needed – sufficient courage to discuss with the common man his right to that participation."*
> Freire (1974)

One of Freire's central educational concepts is *conscientização*, which he defines as "learning to perceive social, political and economic contradictions, and to take action against the oppressive elements of reality". Central to this is an active dialogue within an empathetic relationship; communication and intercommunication between teacher and pupils that "creates a critical attitude. It is nourished by love, humility, hope, faith and trust."

Freire contrasts this to an anti-dialogical approach which, in the absence of empathy, is based on communiques rather than communication. This critical consciousness – the ability to see contradictions and address them – allows people to become responsible subjects as opposed to objects. It encourages the understanding of reality, and the capacity to look at a problem and seek correlations and causality in order to act in a consistent and cohesive manner. It is an ongoing process that seeks to understand things as they exist empirically and are able to be manipulated.

It's important to note that Freire is not anti-theory or content. His objection is to verbalism – words and thought lacking in action. He was equally scathing about action with a lack of thought. He sees the need for theory in terms of contemplation linked to action, not the "erroneous connotation of abstraction or opposition to reality". Dialogue allows communication and hence reflection on the world but, to be authentic, dialogue must lead to actions: "there is no transformation without action". Naming injustice is insufficient unless that naming leads to the injustice being addressed. This is particularly relevant given the Black Lives Matter movement and general lack of equality for people from BAME backgrounds.

Decolonising the curriculum is an important part of curriculum reform. Clarity about the content that needs to be taught must be matched by clarity about the reason for teaching it. Purpose is of paramount importance. If the aim of the curriculum change is to address the injustice, the focus needs to be on personal empowerment. This is what Biesta (2015) refers to as "subjectification", Freire's term for being known and able to act, rather than being an object to be acted on. The curriculum needs to lead to and support thoughtful actions, including its own development, that will remove discrimination, address inequalities and improve equity. This is different from socialisation, which would seek to develop an understanding and initiation into African, Asian or other minority ethnic cultures. For black communities, this would include a sense of connection to and with the African diaspora. Socialisation helps to give a sense of who we are through our shared heritage. Alternatively, the aim of the curriculum could be focused on the acquisition of knowledge about particular people, events or actions, including the slave trade and its abolition or the partition of India. The knowledge may be used to help gain a particular qualification.

These three aims are not mutually exclusive and may be seen as interdependent. The key is being clear about the purpose(s) behind any curricular change, not simply defining the content to be covered.

Freire's educational approach is intrinsically linked with building communities and overcoming social, political, economic or cultural disadvantage. In essence, his work on personal empowerment and social transformation was "preparation for citizenship", one of the other main philosophies of education. It was also related to preparation for the world of work. He considered political freedom as linked to economic development and personal financial security, "thereby ending the oppressive power of the rich over the very poor". The poorer the community, the truer this becomes. This call for work that pays a fair wage co-exists with the call for dignity.

> *" ... their work is not the price they pay for being men but rather a way of loving – and of helping the world to be a better place."*
> Freire (1974)

> *"They must realise that they are fighting not merely for freedom from hunger but for ... freedom to create and to construct, to wonder and to venture."* Freire (2017)

If you've ever had the privilege of listening to the education consultant David Cameron (@realdcameron) call for "a revolution of common sense" at an educational conference, you may well have heard him belt out the lyrics to the strike song *Bread and Roses*:

> *"As we go marching, marching*
> *We battle too for men*
> *For they are women's children*
> *And we mother them again*
> *Our lives shall not be sweated*
> *From birth until life closes*
> *Hearts starve as well as bodies*
> *Give us bread, but give us roses."*

The line "Give us bread, but give us roses" originates from a speech given by Rose Schneiderman, an American labour union leader. The speech was linked to a strike, led mainly by women working in the textile industry, in the early 20th century. Its objective was to gain enhanced pay (bread) and dignified working conditions (roses).

In education, many see the power imbalance in the accountability system but also its wider impact. The stresses and pressures of an audit and surveillance culture are transferred from the system outside schools to the culture inside them. A life well lived applies to the staff who work in our schools as well as to children and young people. If schools and their leaders are not clear and explicit about their purpose, there is the potential for misalignment. External pressures begin to define us. Culture and consistency suffer.

But when educational purpose aligns with our inner purpose, there is a sense of flow. We find our work interesting and satisfying. Where the opposite is true, we become demotivated and in the worse cases disillusioned, seeking our purpose outside education. Poor teacher retention is currently inhibiting our work to improve schools. It is critical that purpose is enacted in practice.

Too often we try to do everything. We seek to please too many masters as our level and sense of empowerment drops. The quality of what we do declines, as does the quality of our relationships with family, friends and even ourselves. We don't like the people we have become.

For *Liminal Leadership*, I composed three letters to myself that punctuated the book: one to myself as I started teaching (aged 23), one to myself as I became a headteacher (aged 37) and another to myself as I became CEO of a multi-academy trust (aged 53). Each letter followed a common structure, with the final paragraph always reflecting on the impact of work on my home life. This is the final paragraph from the third letter; I often use it when speaking at conferences:

"You have a great passion for education and your work but don't forget your growing family and wife. Remember the Saturday morning walking with Cath as she was telling you about a book she was reading. It was a true story of a lady with a chronic illness and her workaholic husband. The woman had written about how her husband's passion has been his work. 'I wish I'd been your passion' will haunt you. Cath will spend half her evenings married to you as a downstairs widow whilst you work away on school business upstairs; these things matter but so do she and the family."

The unspoken lament within the paragraph is that much of the time I spent upstairs was wasted. Too much of what I did made no real difference to the life chances of the children and young people in our schools. I can never have that time back. Now, I have the opportunity to reset my home/work balance so I have time for my family (my greatest passion) and time to do some work well. Both contribute to giving me purpose in life.

What is also left unspoken is that, as a school leader, I implemented a whole set of unnecessary plans and objectives that affected the workload of staff. This in turn impacted on their home lives and relationships. Positions of authority are primarily about responsibility, not power.

The book *It Doesn't Have to be Crazy at Work* (2018) by Jason Fried and David Heinemeier Hansson led me to reflect on my blog about taking back control. If we want empowered young people in our classrooms then we need empowered people in our staffrooms. They work together or not at all. I have reproduced my blog post here:

PUTTING THE 'HOME' BACK INTO YOUR HOME/WORK BALANCE

People are now increasingly talking about a home/work instead of a work/life balance. Work is part of my life but has too often intruded into the home part. I struggled to leave the worry at work and can be slightly obsessed with answering emails. Twitter isn't really part of my work but is another distraction that means my phone is never far from my side. I'm my own worst enemy.

The good news about being your own worst enemy is that you have it within your gift to do something about it. If you are a leader, it is within your gift and it is also your responsibility to ensure you carefully manage the workload of others. Reducing workload – getting rid of the unnecessary and unproductive; focusing on what works and what matters – is an ongoing challenge.

What works and what matters?
If you want to have more hours to spend on your home life you will simply have to start doing fewer things. The upside of doing fewer things is that you can really focus on them, doing them much better. The list of debunked educational ideas is growing by the day; school leaders and teachers need to act collectively to remove them from daily practice. For example, we've never done annual performance-related pay; it is a waste of time and energy. At a classroom level, many teachers are over-marking and under-planning, often due to daft school marking requirements. Collecting copious amounts of unreliable data about teachers and pupils – the cursed six-weekly data drop – has become a national obsession.

Doing nothing is an option (don't be told otherwise)
"No is easier to do, yes is easier to say" is one of my favourite quotes from *It Doesn't Have to be Crazy at Work*. It's similar to my "More noes equals better yeses". It can feel rather unfriendly and potentially isolating to say no to new ideas and initiatives. However, saying yes to everything is the first step towards personal burnout and organisational chaos. Not everything is equally important. Separate the educational wheat from the chaff. Reject more than you commit to. "There is only so much time" has to become a mantra and way of life.

Equally, sometimes things *are* important but you just don't currently have the time; kick them down the line to next year. It's a "wait" or a "later" rather than an absolute no. Don't operate from fear of missing out. There is a difference between busyness and effectiveness. Being a late adopter has its benefits.

Recognise your stress behaviours
When I am stressed and chasing my tail, I always pile more and more meetings into my diary or tasks on to each day's to-do list. For a long time, I didn't realise that I did this; now I can spot myself starting to work in this way and control my impulsive behaviours.

My response now is threefold. Firstly, what is not really a priority? These just get deleted. Secondly, what is urgent and what can be delayed to next week or next month? Thirdly, what meetings are unnecessary for me to attend (including ones I may have organised)? These I delete from my diary. One year, when I was particularly fed up with the meetings organised by the local authority, I sent my apologies to every single one. I eventually got rumbled but had one of the best years as a leader in my career. Read the minutes of meetings and you'll catch up with the important bits and realise you didn't miss a lot.

Be ruthless and organised

You need a systematic way to stay on top of things; mine is an electronic diary and to-do list with the corresponding apps. I wish Google would actually integrate their calendar and tasks into one app, a bit like they've done with the desktop version. My Gmail strategy is to delete most emails without opening them; you can usually spot the rubbish early. I unsubscribe from as many marketing ones as possible. I open and respond immediately to some and close others as "unread" if I need a bit more thinking or action time. Everything in one place is key for me.

Immediate responses are not required

The downside of my strategy is that I tend to have my Gmail, calendar and task lists open all the time on my desktop. There is a tendency to check and respond frequently, including regularly checking my phone when I'm away from work. Although the speed of my response can be impressive to some, it leads to me receiving more emails and the downward spiral continues. Some people have set times when they respond to emails, giving themselves long stretches of uninterrupted time to focus on the big stuff.

Time slots

Zarraga's rule was incorrectly explained to me when I was timetabling: put all your messy bits of the timetable into one slot. You need to think about this when dealing with the multiple tasks you complete on a daily basis. Some things can be done quickly; others require more extended thought and time to complete. I've fallen into the trap of working in small time slots: 15 minutes here and 20 minutes there, then another 10 and 15 minutes later in the day, repeated the following day and the day after. What was a job that required 60-90 minutes of focused work has now taken twice as long and been spread across three days. In between, numerous emails were answered and conversations snatched as I flitted from one thing to another.

Far better to apportion all the bits of jobs to an hour a day and allow longer slots, with emails and the phone switched off, to complete the important cognitively demanding jobs. On days when I don't have much time, I don't timetable many tasks – they simply won't get done.

Leave perfection to God; good is good enough

In *Liminal Leadership*, I wrote about the moment Father Luiz suggested we leave perfection to God (that's his/her/their job) and how it hit home hard. I'm a bit of a perfectionist and can literally waste hours polishing and perfecting things that were already more than fit for purpose, driving other people mad at the same time. As I've aged and hopefully matured, I've also realised that my idea of perfection, like everyone else's, is largely idiosyncratic. Before starting larger tasks, think about how good is good enough and complete it to that standard. I literally would have worked thousands of hours less if I had fully thought things through.

Work time must balance with downtime

There is a need to recharge batteries or, as I sometimes say, "refill the reservoir" if we are not to become exhausted. When exhausted, we are no use at work and no good at home; we become diminished as people. I am thinking about removing the Gmail app from my phone at weekends and during holidays. I am only *thinking* about it, as it seems a huge step. The other option would be to show a bit more self-control when not at work. As I use the camera on my phone quite a bit, the temptation to take a sneaky look at emails is always there!

Hardly any of the emails I receive are an emergency. Urgent issues tend to arrive via phone calls. Maybe it is time to remove those apps after all. They can quickly be reinstated on Sunday evening or first thing Monday morning.

Alignment and coherence

Too many things in classrooms and schools are misaligned. This leads to particularly inefficient ways of working. Our newly qualified teachers (NQTs) have an induction programme, instructional coach (working with them for 20 minutes in the classroom and discussing aspects of practice for 20 minutes outside the classroom each week), a subject mentor and a professional mentor. You could not claim we do not try to look after our NQTs. However, there is a concern that replication or inefficient delivery is wasting people's time. Every now and again, it is worth looking at your systems and processes and realigning them.

Find your own combination of solutions

Our lives are different. Your solutions or combinations of the above will be different to mine. It is important to recognise this while also putting in place some general rules. For example, the move to only sending emails between

7am and 6pm Monday to Friday and never during the holidays (made by the new headteacher at St Mary's Catholic Academy) is a great example. Not everyone appreciated it at the beginning; I doubt any of us would now change it. We have a responsibility towards each other to help people rebalance their lives, not to damage their wellbeing.

In helping to empower adults, removing the oppressive forces of continual audit and surveillance, schools are taking a huge step towards creating a culture with appropriate high levels of autonomy. This is the fertile soil from which agency grows.

CHAPTER 5
Cultural transmission

The cultural transmission philosophy of education is almost exclusively focused on knowledge acquisition and the development of the intellect.

> " ... *culture being a pursuit of our total perfection by means of getting to know, on all the matters which most concern us, the best which has been thought and said in the world, and, through this knowledge, turning a stream of fresh and free thought upon our stock notions and habits ...* "   Arnold (1869)

Ignorance is associated with lacking a defined body of knowledge, not a lack of intellect or capacity to reason. The purpose of this knowledge is to create more informed individuals who, through a shared knowledge, have a means to communicate with each other and can in turn produce a more just and cohesive society. This forms the basis for later work on the importance of cultural literacy.

Matthew Arnold was critical of many establishment organisations of his time – religious and political – for seeking to maintain the status quo through thoughtless conformity. Free trade was supposed to lead to a better economic life but was failing millions of working-class people while benefiting the elite few. Democracy was supposed to deliver a just society but was evidently failing.

Arnold classified this fractured Victorian society into: Barbarians (the landowners, who retained the country's land within their own families, living a life of privileged ease), Philistines (the growing, materialistic middle class; the people running commerce, industry and businesses who showed a disdain for art and the intellect) and, the largest of the three classes, the Populace (the working class, seen as an increasing "threat", rising out of their poverty to do as they liked). His concern was that the individuals who constituted the different classes of the Victorian age all operated out of self-interest – and that needed to be challenged. According to Arnold, this self-interest was owing to ignorance; it was a subjective world view limited by a lack of knowledge and understanding of other classes or contexts.

The Corn Laws may be used as an example of how a lack of understanding of different perspectives was leading to social unrest:

> *"Barbarians want higher prices for the grain that grows on their land to increase their wealth. But the Populace want lower prices for the loaf of bread made from that grain. And the Philistine factory owners fear having to increase wages to workers who could no longer afford a loaf of bread ... none of the three classes understood or acknowledged the needs of the others. Without that mutuality, society was hopelessly locked in civil conflict."* Logan (2012)

Arnold's antidote was greater knowledge – a shared knowledge of different perspectives. Those who understood those different perspectives and brought them forward to critique the problems of the time were considered to be cultured. They were to be found in the three different classes of Victorian society.

> *"[Culture] seeks to do away with classes; to make all live in an atmosphere of sweetness and light, and use ideas, as it uses them itself, freely,—to be nourished and not bound by them.*
> *This is the social idea; and the men of culture are the true apostles of equality. The great men of culture are those who have had a passion for diffusing, for making prevail, for carrying from one end of society to the other, the best knowledge, the best ideas of their time ... "* Arnold (1869)

Enhancing culture required people to embark on "a pursuit of our total perfection" – what Arnold termed their "best self". This striving would include the use of knowledge to critique the current thinking and way of living, with the goal of greater social unity. It was for people who were willing to transcend their current class, in which they were trapped as their "ordinary self", to put the needs of the whole society above their individual or class interests. In this way, they would achieve their best self. People of culture were distinguished by their enhanced knowledge of different perspectives, bringing "the best which has been thought and said in the world" alongside a social conscience.

Arnold's use of language – "sweetness and light", "fresh and free" – is rooted in Greek classical culture, which was associated primarily with beauty: creativity, innovation and spontaneity. His language was deliberate and designed to rebalance Victorian society, which Arnold believed had become overly dominated by attributes of Roman classical culture. This emphasised orthodoxy: efficiency, practicality and law/rules. For Arnold, these two cultures were held in tension and needed to be balanced as part of the "natural order".

Cultural literacy

In the preface of his book *Cultural Literacy* (1988), E.D. Hirsch Jr includes a quote by Samuel Johnson:

> *"There is no matter what children should learn first, any more than what leg you should put into your breeches first. Sir, you may stand disputing which is best to put in first, but in the meantime your backside is bare. Sir, while you stand considering which of two things you should teach your child first, another boy has learned 'em both."*

Hirsch describes the basic goal of education as acculturation, "the transmission to children of the specific information shared by the adults of the group". This is rooted in the requirement for all human communities to be able to effectively communicate with each other. It is what Hirsch calls an anthropological theory of education. In many societies this involves literate forms of communication, associated with reading and writing alongside oral communication.

Literacy involves mastering the effective use of standard literate language, which enables people "to give and receive complex information orally and in writing over time and space". This communication is assisted when we can make assumptions about what other people will know. It requires a shared knowledge and understanding that includes but goes beyond the words and information presented to us. We need to understand the content, context and the linguistic shortcuts used.

According to Hirsch, cultural literacy consists of the basic knowledge that is assumed within communication between people in a particular culture or nation, "a network of information that all competent readers possess". Cultural literacy is considered a primary aim of education, one that should lead to greater economic prosperity, social justice and a more effective democracy. The role of schools is to teach this shared knowledge.

Hirsch's view was that American schools, in failing to directly teach the cultural knowledge required in order to understand and engage in national communication, were doing the greatest disservice to those pupils from disadvantaged backgrounds trapped in a cycle of poverty driven by illiteracy.

Children from more socioeconomically advantaged families are likely to acquire higher levels of literacy owing to interaction with literate parents and their circle of friends. This is a view that has, in part, shaped the narrative around educational changes in England during the past decade, 2010-20.

Hirsch asserts that description, not prescription, is required when seeking to build cultural literacy: "Cultural literacy is represented not by a prescriptive list of books but rather a descriptive list of the information actually possessed by literate Americans." Much of this list is arbitrary, built around accidents of culture, not merit – it is what previous generations have decided was important to retain and pass on. For Hirsch, cultural literacy becomes a critical differentiator between the illiterate and literate; between the advantaged and disadvantaged. Most importantly, it can be taught.

National vocabulary, hence cultural literacy, consists of three elements: knowledge of terms that form part of a shared culture; those needed for literacy in the native language; and the information that is unique or special to the country or culture. Even where nations have a shared language and an overlapping history, they select from that history differently. The curriculum in Scotland may well place a greater emphasis on William Wallace, Bannockburn, Robert the Bruce and Robert Burns than the curriculum in England. The American curriculum would include the Boston Tea Party, Paul Revere, the Founding Fathers and the Constitution.

The total content of cultural literacy is actually quite limited and a large part of the knowledge is stable. Changes usually happen very slowly. Some aspects, like spellings, are essentially static. With the majority of the population having learned an established spelling that is contained in books and other writings, it becomes difficult to change. The effort required is too great compared with the value of any outcome. This, in part, explains the conservative nature of the knowledge that constitutes cultural literacy. Hirsch calculated that 80% of the knowledge was 100 years old or more. The stability of this knowledge assists schools, allowing time to determine the curriculum, plan and sequence its delivery and evaluate the impact. The national dimension creates an overlay with how education is organised in many parts of the world.

While cultural literacy might change slowly, there are also times of dynamic change: "lockdown", "social distancing" and "flattening the curve" have recently been added to our lexicon. It is interesting to consider how these terms and their usage might evolve over time. To what extent might "flattening the curve" become shorthand for behaviour aimed at averting an undesirable or potentially disastrous situation, even when there is no appropriate graphical representation? Or might "lockdown" become used to denote a course of action that accepts short-term pain/restrictions for longer term gain? "Social distancing", in time, might be used to convey a sense of people working together for the common good. If it does, then for those who did not experience the Covid-19 pandemic, the use of the word "distancing" would be an unusual juxtaposition to give a sense of people working together.

Literacy in schools

When we looked at literacy across our multi-academy trust, different issues were identified in the primary and secondary schools. The breadth of the primary curriculum had been narrowed, ironically in an attempt to improve pupils' literacy skills. What was also revealed was the very limited range of literature being read by pupils. Their diet consisted mainly of books by Dahl, Walliams and Morpurgo.

However, what took me by greater surprise was whether pupils were reading in class with their teacher at all. What I thought would be a given, in every primary classroom, was in fact hugely variable. A survey by Teacher Tapp in November 2018 makes similar findings. The survey question is very specific – "Do you [the teacher] read a book aloud to your class?" – and it may be that pupils read silently or to each other, but the results are still a wake-up call. The drop off in reading "every day" after Reception is quite staggering and not what I had expected.

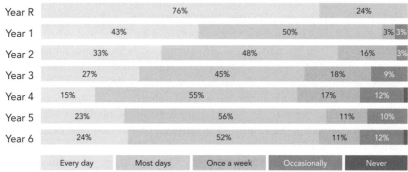

(Source: Teacher Tapp, 2018)

There will never be universal agreement about which 30 books every child should read while at primary school. Even the idea is contentious. In developing a literary canon, a school can emphasise the local, national or the international, as it believes appropriate. The books can be biased towards deepening an understanding of its own community or different communities. The canon we decided on across our trust's two primary academies is currently:

- **Year 1:** *The Storm Whale; What the Ladybird Heard; After the Fall; Tidy; Winnie and Wilbur in Winter; Dave the Lonely Monster; The Lighthouse Keeper's Lunch; The Squirrels Who Squabbled.*
- **Year 2:** *Jumanji; Aesop's Funky Fables; The Owl Who Was Afraid of the Dark; Fantastic Mr Fox; The Dragonsitter; The Worst Witch.*
- **Year 3:** *The Hodgeheg; Ice Palace; Woof!; The Iron Man; The Butterfly Lion.*
- **Year 4:** *The Firework-Maker's Daughter; Perry Angel's Suitcase; The Turbulent Term of Tyke Tiler; Emil and the Detectives; The Legend of Podkin One-Ear.*
- **Year 5:** *Journey to Jo'burg; The Midnight Fox; Wonder; Five Children and It; Millions.*
- **Year 6:** *Holes; Skellig; The Wolves of Willoughby Chase; Cogheart; A Monster Calls; A Little History of the World* (illustrated, non-fiction).

Each class also reads a selection of non-fiction texts, using either the DK *First Children's Encyclopedia* or the DK *Children's Illustrated Encyclopedia*. Morning literacy lessons make increasing use of texts that are linked to the reading canon. For example, the reading of *Cogheart* is preceded by an account written by a schoolboy after a Zeppelin attack on London in World War I, plus an accompanying video. A text on the Chihuahuan Desert gives pupils an understanding of the climate the young prisoners in *Holes* have to suffer.

A reader's background knowledge helps them to understand a text. Daniel Willingham (2017) confirms that readers make greater sense, or any sense, of a text when they have the background knowledge to support an understanding of what is written. Deliberately expanding this understanding, through a range of texts, helps to build cultural literacy.

The common reader

Cultural knowledge is that possessed by the "common reader". It exists above the level of knowledge that everyone might possess but below that of the specialist. Hirsch (1988) explains this with reference to how people read or communicate orally: they gain a general impression of what is being communicated, rather than remember the detail. Using the analogy of a compass, Hirsch proposed:

> " ... we must draw a northerly border, above which lies specialized knowledge, and a southerly one, below which lies knowledge so obvious and widely known that its inclusion would make the list unusually long ... To the east lie materials that are still too new to have passed into general currency ... To the west are items ... which have passed from view and are now known only to older generations."

If a teacher said, "It was a horrible wet lunchtime. The rain and wind were coming in horizontally from the Irish Sea. My Year 9 afternoon lesson was like Armageddon," we would understand that the lesson had not gone well. In fact, it had been a bit of a battle. We deliberately select from the sentence what we consider to be the core message: that it had been a difficult lesson. The weather, possible location, year group and timing of the lesson are all secondary to the term Armageddon, which conveys the main meaning or the gist of the sentence.

At a common level of knowledge, Armageddon is understood to be a battle or conflict; that is sufficient to convey and understand the message within the sentence. At a more specialised level, some people may know that the term is found in the New Testament, the Book of Revelation, and refers to the last battle between good and evil before the Day of Judgement. This specialist knowledge adds nothing to our understanding of what is being communicated by the teacher. Cultural literacy is a general knowledge that aids us in communicating in an effective and efficient manner.

Hirsch sees the alternative as an unshared extensive curriculum that would leave the poorest pupils at a disadvantage. He considers progressive styles of skills-based education as illusory, because these approaches fail to take into account the factual knowledge and understanding upon which literacy is based. According to Hirsch, there is a paradox in the inherent conservatism of cultural literacy: "We make social and economic progress only by teaching myths and facts that are predominantly traditional."

Stressing the importance and impact of a shared extensive curriculum, he asks those people engaging in the debate to:

> " ... *keep clearly in view the high stakes involved in their deliberation: breaking the cycle of illiteracy for deprived children; raising the living standard of families who have been illiterate; making our country more competitive in international markets; achieving greater social justice; enabling all citizens to participate in the political process.*" Hirsch (1988)

If people are able to communicate and deliberate with each other then they can make important collective decisions. This is the basis of the democratic process and the argument for cultural literacy leading to a more effective democracy. It is expressed succinctly by Thomas Carlyle: "I do not believe in the collective wisdom of individual ignorance." Or by Isaac Asimov: " ... the false notion that democracy means that 'my ignorance is just as good as your knowledge'."

Hirsch urges clarity about educational priorities, as "educational policy always involves choices between degrees of worthiness". He is unequivocal that cultural literacy, set at a national level, is of paramount importance and needs to be prioritised partly because the curriculum is "the most important controllable influence" on educational outcomes, including literacy.

In echoes of Arnold, Hirsch's concern is that although pupils may know a great deal of knowledge, it is narrowly confined to their own generation and context. Their embodied cultural capital is derived too much from their peer group, community or family, and too little from their education. Hirsch addresses this balancing act between personal and shared culture, saying of the latter: " ... it excludes nobody; it cuts across generations and social groups and classes; it is not usually one's first culture, but it should be everyone's second, existing as it does beyond the narrow spheres of family, neighbourhood and religion."

There is something deeply alluring in the idea that literacy is a critical differentiator between those who are advantaged and disadvantaged. However, enhanced literacy will only ever be part of the solution. *The Prosecutor*, a book by Nazir Afzal, a former chief prosecutor, exposes the reality of honour killings, domestic violence, sexual abuse and human trafficking; how justice and protection in the law is far more secure and certain for the privileged. Women, people from BAME backgrounds and the poorer in socioeconomic terms are far less protected – their cries are not heard. Overcoming discrimination and long-term disadvantage requires so much more than people being literate. An uncritical approach to the teaching of literacy may do harm.

The vocabulary of a culture is captured in its stories, books and education systems. Hirsch coordinated a list of approximately 5,000 words, sayings, people and dates that form the lexicon of a literate person. The small group of people supporting Hirsch in putting together the list "gave priority to words and phrases found in the front pages and editorial columns of *serious* newspapers and in the pages of *serious* books and magazines" (Hirsch, 1988). The emphasis in the previous sentence is mine. It seeks to make the point that selecting from culture is open to bias.

Although data about the words and terms that feature in the list could be presented objectively, decisions around what constitutes a "serious" publication, as opposed to a popular one, are not objective. Personally, I would consider *The Times*, *The Financial Times* and *The Guardian* to be serious newspapers. I wouldn't consider *The Sun* to be one, but its circulation is approximately twice the combined circulation of the three other papers. The possibility of cultural imposition, including by omission, is very real.

In looking at the delivery of cultural literacy, the compromise Hirsch sees is a curriculum that is traditional in content but varied in terms of the pedagogy and the materials used. The key is providing pupils with a "common core of cultural information". This would form the extensive curriculum – the shared traditional information. Hirsch's proposal was that there should be a shared extensive curriculum for all pupils from kindergarten to eighth grade; this equates to Reception to Year 9 in the English education system. It would form an aspect but would not be the entirety of a child's education. By agreeing the content of the list for each year group and a sequence or number of thoughtful sequences, literacy would be substantially improved.

Alongside this would sit a second component: the intensive curriculum. Hirsch's intensive curriculum, with its more specialised knowledge, can create a different curriculum structure to that required by cultural literacy. This specialised and systematic knowledge is organised in disciplines, branches of academic study that "represent powerful – and qualitatively different – ways of thinking about the world" (Wiliam, 2013). This way of thinking – disciplinary habits of mind – creates rigour within a curriculum. It helps to explain the very different curriculum approaches often seen in primary and secondary schools.

The intensive curriculum, while equally essential, would differ from cultural literacy in that it would provide greater flexibility and choice to individual pupils, teachers and schools. It would also be studied to far greater depth, providing specialised knowledge relevant to the individual pupils. Hirsch's view was that the extensive and intensive curriculums could work alongside each other without the need to impose an "arbitrary core curriculum". This contrasts with the current curriculum requirements in England, particularly with respect to the choice available at GCSE.

CHAPTER 6

Formation of the subject-based curriculum

The English education system evolved over time (Williams, 2011, pp.153-169). From the late sixth century, grammar schools were established, linked to cathedrals and monasteries, to teach Latin and to train and prepare priests and monks to read scripture aloud (rhetoric). By the 12th century, the curriculum had expanded to form the seven liberal arts: the foundational trivium of grammar, rhetoric and dialectic, and the quadrivium of music, arithmetic, geometry and astronomy. This curriculum formed the basis for the specialised study of law, medicine and theology.

By the 18th century, a post-Enlightenment Europe had moved into the Age of Reason. The school curriculum began to change significantly, for the first time in centuries. Dissenting academies were established with a curriculum that included mathematics, geography, modern languages and, crucially, the physical sciences. The modern school curriculum was beginning to take shape.

During the 19th century, additional subjects were added to the curriculum, including natural sciences, history, drawing and music. With the formation of local education authorities at the beginning of the 20th century, education at a secondary level consisted of a four-year course "leading to a certificate, in English language and literature, geography, history, a language other than English, mathematics, science, drawing, manual work, physical training, and household crafts for girls" (Williams, 2011). Those first six subjects form the current subject-based English Baccalaureate. With subjects at the core of today's secondary curriculum, and increasingly the primary curriculum, there is a direct association between primary, secondary and higher education that drives the system and the purpose underpinning it. Schooling has increasingly become about preparation for university studies.

Powerful knowledge

Young (2014) defines "powerful knowledge" using two basic assumptions: firstly, that there are different types of knowledge (for example, that gained from everyday experience as opposed to that contained within different curriculum subjects) and, secondly, that there is better knowledge. The term "better knowledge" is linked to structure and purpose; it is not about whether there is knowledge that is inherently good or bad.

Whereas knowledge from everyday experience is linked to the context in which it was acquired, subject knowledge is context-independent. Subject knowledge enables pupils to move beyond their current experiences, acquiring new ideas or underpinning concepts that may be transferred and used in other appropriate contexts. The power of subject knowledge is that it helps pupils to envisage alternatives; to predict, to explain and to think in new ways.

Powerful knowledge is specialised and systematic. Based on the work of specialist communities, it has been developed "with a well-defined focus and relatively fixed boundaries" (Young, 2014). These boundaries create the necessary separation that enables appropriate aspects of different disciplinary knowledge to become incorporated into discrete subjects within the curriculum. Powerful knowledge is also systematic. Its concepts are linked in an intentional way to create a coherent body of associated knowledge.

Christine Counsell (2018) provides detail that is of importance to teachers and the teaching of knowledge. In particular, she focuses on the character of knowledge, "its structure, its origins, its status as a set of truth claims (such as their revisability) and the relationships of teachers and pupils to that knowledge". Knowledge is the start of the process of inducting pupils into the specialist communities formed around the academic study of a particular discipline.

Differentiating between substantive and disciplinary knowledge (the former consisting of what would be taught as established facts, while the latter concerns the establishment of that knowledge, the certainty with which it is held and how it continues to be revised), Counsell draws important distinctions between different subjects. She contrasts the teaching of history and science within schools. Scholarship in history involves "the social process of claim and counter-claim". Using the Treaty of Versailles, she explains that although historians agree about dates and events, "attributions of cause, consequences or significance ... are not givens" and are open to argument. However, at a school level, science places a far greater emphasis on the teaching of substantive knowledge. There are far more givens. Although pupils will study the scientific method, conduct investigations and consider errors and degrees of uncertainty, the conclusions they will need to reach have already been established by the scientific community.

The different balance of substantive and disciplinary knowledge in each subject has implications for both pedagogy and assessment. To what extent does the subject require pupils to be able to produce or reproduce knowledge? Counsell emphasises the need "for pupils to learn how knowledge is formed and changed". Without this disciplinary knowledge, the curriculum, rather than consisting of powerful knowledge, will be one that is "merely ossifying a canon". Counsell refers to the knowledge-rich curriculum as usually being associated with substantive knowledge (the knowledge that pupils will need to remember).

Tom Sherrington (2018) provides a more detailed set of principles for the knowledge-rich curriculum that sees both the knowledge content and the subject's traditions as underpinning philosophies. In addition, the content must be specified in detail, sequenced and mapped deliberately and coherently, and taught to be remembered, not merely encountered.

Planning the subject curriculum

The planning of the curriculum to ensure the intellectual development of the child, as described above, is a long-term labour of professional love. There are no short cuts. It takes significant time, professional knowledge and understanding, and can be supported by agreed processes (ways of working) and shared language.

Teaching and learning planner

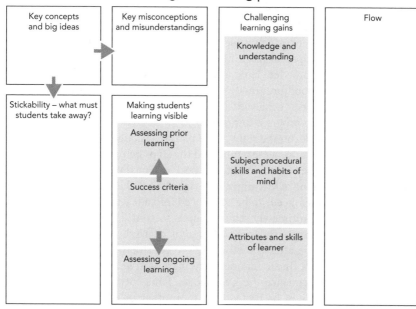

In seeking to ensure that progression was one of the key aspects of the curriculum across our trust, we highlighted the importance of developing both surface and deeper learning, using the types of knowledge identified in Bloom's revised taxonomy (factual, conceptual, procedural and metacognitive). This involved the sequencing of the curriculum (the "what") with a common process of informed collaborative planning and evaluation (the "how").

Significant departmental/phase-specific time was made available across the trust. This gave teachers the opportunity to plan together and share expertise, with respect to the content and how it might best be implemented in the classroom. The proforma/planner on the previous page dates from about 2014/15 and was used by teachers across the trust for collaborative planning.

As with any potential proforma, it is too easy to see this as a set of boxes to fill, rather than a set of questions that should be pondered and discussed with others when planning the curriculum. It starts in the top corner on the left-hand side, flowing down and to the right in an iterative process.

The first set of questions is about end points and road blocks. What is the key understanding you want pupils to acquire during this topic, module or series of lessons? What kind of errors have pupils made in the past when being taught this content? Part of the discussion around common errors or misconceptions would be how to avoid them being made in the first place and how to address them if they are. The "stickability" (a term originally used by Ross Morrison McGill @TeacherToolkit) refers to the core content that must be retained and retrieved by pupils, as future learning will require it and build upon it.

"Making students' learning visible" is a straight take from Hattie (2009) and forms part of the reciprocal teaching approach identified by Wiliam as a key aspect of classroom practice. How will you assess what pupils already know? What indicators of good progress will you be looking for? And how will you know if these have been achieved? It is partly about defining excellence and partly about assessing progress towards it.

The final two blocks on the right of the planner ask questions relating to the balance of surface and deeper learning and the steps being taken to develop the pupil as a learner. They form part of the check on "challenge" – is the learning expected in this scheme of learning about right (the Goldilocks principle)? This expected learning then needs to be sequenced into a teaching flow.

Although we will ultimately require pupils to consider a number of pieces of knowledge simultaneously, in order to construct schema, we have to teach these sequentially, one after the other, before considering them together. We necessarily teach in a linear manner, but there is frequently more than one appropriate way to sequence the knowledge. Time spent discussing this and why one sequence might be preferential to another or equally valid is a key aspect of professional development. Too often it is overlooked in the busyness of all the other requirements placed on schools.

Overall, the planner is focused on teacher clarity: understanding what needs to be taught; how best to sequence it or whether various sequences are equally valid; what must be retained by the pupils for future learning to be effective; and what success would look like. It is also about creating a shared process and language for teachers to plan together.

CHAPTER 7
Preparation for work

In the preparation for work philosophy of education, the focus is on problem-solving and real-world experiences. As more educated workers are more productive, there is a correlation between educational achievement and economic prosperity.

In an episode of the *Classroom 101* podcast (tinyurl.com/y9ww646n), Laura McInerney recounts the story of Kate Adie, the BBC's former chief news correspondent. Adie covered many disasters and conflicts in her career and spent time in numerous war zones, sometimes buffered by UN peacekeepers. In one incident, Adie was able to put her knowledge of the Swedish language, gained through her degree in Scandinavian studies, to good use with Swedish peacekeeping troops. A degree in Scandinavian studies and the ability to speak Swedish are pretty niche outcomes of a university education in England, yet they proved invaluable to Adie. Serendipitous is the word that springs to mind.

Powerful knowledge in a disciplinary sense is subject to debate. Powerful knowledge in life – that which will matter in terms of a person's economic (or, in Adie's case, personal) wellbeing – is difficult, if not impossible, to predict beyond basic literacy and numeracy. From a curriculum-planning perspective, this is problematic. The knowledge needed varies from person to person and is not known in advance. Schools also can't account for shifts in the career choices made by people over time. It is impossible to build a curriculum for a particular young person with hindsight.

This has periodically led to calls for transferable skills to be taught. These calls are often rejected from a subject-based perspective. The habits of mind (ways of thinking) associated with disciplinary knowledge are intrinsically tied to the substantive knowledge – the established facts. Transferring generic skills between subjects is unhelpful. Solving problems in maths can require the use of assumptions, whereas in science it is more likely to require the control and isolation of variables.

However, there is a set of skills that may usefully be transferred between contexts. Although these skills need a context and content in order to be practised, they are more suited to transfer. The transferrable skills identified by businesses often include: good communication skills; the ability to work in teams, problem-solve and lead a team; project management skills at a personal and organisational level, including the ability to manage time; digital, information and data management skills; and a strong work ethic. What is seen by businesses as essential is arguably marginalised in our current curriculum models. That is a choice rather than a necessity. Changing this requires a proportion of the curriculum to sit outside the constraints inherent in a subject-based model.

When working with post-16 students and, more infrequently, Year 9 pupils on the Extended Project Qualification, I would often teach them about various project management skills and tools. Hopefully, many of them will remember the Gantt chart that I would insist they produced, monitored and evaluated. I have used such a tool in my personal and professional life when managing or leading major projects. It has always proved invaluable.

Alongside the potential to develop a transferable toolkit for young people, there is also the need to allow them to pursue particular courses that align with their current career aspirations. Most schools seem more adept and comfortable doing this when the chosen career pathway is academic rather than vocational or occupational.

There are implications for allowing informed decision-making by young people on following particular courses that are of greater interest to them or may be orientated towards a certain job market or vocational/occupational career. Making curriculum time available for these choices has an impact upon the size of any core curriculum. The disciplines and subjects that are orientated towards further academic study, often at university, are held in tension with the time required for more vocational/occupational studies. This tension is further influenced by our country's perception of vocational and occupational qualifications and work. In England, these are often perceived as being second class compared with work accessed through a university degree. The argument is often framed in terms of concerns over disproportionately higher numbers of disadvantaged pupils being directed towards vocational and occupational courses.

Yet despite these challenges, it is reasonable to expect that schools will make a contribution to the economic prosperity of the country through preparing young people for work.

"Schematically one can say that a child must be taught, first, the accepted behaviour and values of his society; second, the general

knowledge and attitudes appropriate to an educated man; and, third, a particular skill by which he will earn his living and contribute to the welfare of his society."
Williams (2011, first published in 1961)

Raymond Williams' third element, relating to the role of schools in preparing young people for work and contributing to society, was also a key element of the Ruskin College speech given in October 1976 by the Labour prime minister James Callaghan. This launched the Great Debate about the nature and purpose of public education. Callaghan proposed that education had two goals: "to equip children to the best of their ability for a lively, constructive, place in society, and also to fit them to do a job of work". His speech signalled politicians' desire to influence the education system at a level previously unseen or even imagined. But this political influence hasn't always been consistent with preparing young people for the variety of opportunities available in the workplace.

This can best be exemplified by the attempts to introduce or impose the English Baccalaureate (EBacc) in/on schools in England. The English Baccalaureate sits within the cultural transmission philosophy of education – more specifically, a subject-based curriculum. It might be appropriate in terms of preparing people for work (as long as that work is predicated on the purely intellectual) but it proves limiting on more vocational and occupational roles, as well as personal empowerment. There are not many choices for pupils to make in an English Baccalaureate key stage 4 curriculum.

The English Baccalaureate sits at an extreme owing to three dimensions: the number of pupils expected to study it (90% by 2025), the amount of curriculum time it occupies and the subjects included within it. It is enforced by Ofsted's latest inspection framework and performance tables. Section 162 of the current education inspection framework contains what I refer to as the Great Colon (see the first sentence):

"At the heart of an effective key stage 4 curriculum is a strong academic core: the EBacc. The government's response to its EBacc consultation, published in July 2017, confirmed that the large majority of pupils should be expected to study the EBacc. It is therefore the government's national ambition that 75% of Year 10 pupils in state-funded mainstream schools should be starting to study EBacc GCSE courses nationally by 2022 (taking their examinations in 2024), rising to 90% by 2025 (taking their examinations in 2027)." Ofsted (2019)

My use of the phrase "the Great Colon" is based on a reflection by Father Richard Rohr, who notes that the Apostles' Creed has a comma between the statements "born of the Virgin Mary, suffered under Pontius Pilate". The time between Jesus' birth and death is covered by this single comma, termed the Great Comma. There is a yawning gap with important detail missing.

Similarly, there is a yawning gap in thinking about alternative key stage 4 possibilities, with implications for how young people are prepared for work. The English Baccalaureate is merely an example of an academic curriculum rather than what is being proposed; namely, it is at the "heart of an effective key stage 4 curriculum". The English Baccalaureate occupies 70-80% of time in key stage 4, depending on the time given to English and maths. A further 10% is likely to be required for PE, PSHE, citizenship and religious studies. This leaves time for one or at the most two options for pupils.

Standard English Baccalaureate curriculum

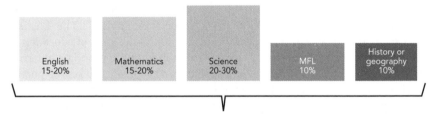

The EBacc occupies 70-90% of key stage 4 curriculum time

Greater time and more options could be created by having a smaller core consisting of English, maths and science. Some would be concerned at the loss of the modern foreign languages element, which will not achieve the 90% required by 2025 owing to a chronic lack of MFL teachers, and others the lack of history or geography. However, these two elements are arguably more questionable within the core curriculum.

The story goes that the English Baccalaureate and the subjects within it were made up for an appearance by Michael Gove, then the education secretary, on the BBC's *Andrew Marr Show* in 2010. This partly explains why some of the subjects changed over the first few weeks, but not why religious studies is omitted as a humanity. Aspects of the list are idiosyncratic. There is an argument to be made from a disciplinary perspective that MFL and English language have elements in common. The absences of the arts and technology, with their different disciplinary traditions, are notable and some groups have suggested that the English Baccalaureate should be extended to include them. This would run the risk of further limiting time for work-related learning.

The exclusion of religious education from the list of English Baccalaureate subjects was particularly galling and problematic for us, as a Catholic school. There is a requirement for 10% of curriculum time to be given to the study of RE. This limits curriculum flexibility at key stage 4. Beyond this, RE is such a powerful subject. It asks the big questions in life – it is about both the "I" and "we" of humanity – and it promotes spiritual, moral, social and cultural development, and understanding of individuals and diverse communities.

Unsurprisingly, our pupils were always going to study Christianity as one of their two major world religions. Studying Judaism would provide them with a historic root from which to develop a greater understanding of Christianity, as well as a greater awareness of the many challenges faced by the Jewish people over time. Alternatively, the study of Islam would create an important connection to Christianity and unpick many current misunderstandings. Coverage in the news is often associated with terrorism and atrocities. This is not the Islam or Islamic community I grew increasingly to understand and respect during eight years teaching in Blackburn.

It is sad to see in too many secondary schools that RE has become a Cinderella subject compared with history and geography. There is no good reason. Rather, it is an inappropriate imposition by the powerful few on the many. The English Baccalaureate was never fit for purpose. It was the wrong solution to the problem of high-stakes accountability and high-tariff vocational subjects. There are alternative curriculum approaches that could be taken.

Evolving out of work by Headteachers' Roundtable, led by Tom Sherrington, the National Baccalaureate Trust proposes a model that would involve core learning (based on the current qualifications framework), a personal project (often utilising the level 2 and 3 Extended Project Qualification) and a personal development challenge. At level 3, the personal development challenge would consist of 100-150 hours over Years 12 and 13. Schools would have flexibility over its exact composition, with one defining the areas as community, physical, cultural and creative, with a minimum of 15 hours in each area. These could be delivered via recognised programmes: Duke of Edinburgh's Award, National Citizen Service, World Challenge, Outward Bound or the Community Sports Leadership Award. Level 2 would require 85 hours, with another school defining the compulsory components as stewardship, leadership, cultural and creative. If the personal project and personal development challenge became a core element of the curriculum – ensuring an entitlement for all – then some of the more transferrable skills sought by businesses would more likely be developed.

As part of this philosophy of education, there is also a far greater interest in developing links with businesses across a range of curriculum subjects and promoting subjects that have a more vocational orientation. Numerous examples exist: media, health and social care, engineering, leisure and tourism, catering. This can only be achieved by a reduction in the number of subjects studied by pupils as part of a core curriculum. Time is finite, curriculum tensions are inexorable.

CHAPTER 8
Preparation for citizenship

This philosophy focuses on the school's context and seeks to support the development of social capital within families and the local community. Key to its success is ensuring that young people are sufficiently well informed about substantive and current issues, so they can make decisions in support of the democratic process.

Looking back, the difference between the resources and wider services available to support children and families during my first decade of leadership in Blackpool (2000-10) and my second decade (2010-19) is stark. The provision of speech and language therapists, educational psychologists, youth workers and police community support officers disappeared, to a very large extent.

Laura McInerney (2020) charts these stark changes, starting from when Michael Gove "set fire to almost every initiative related to children's wellbeing". She stresses, "Education was never the sole focus of schools, and it's a shame it has taken a pandemic to prove it." McInerney describes how school leaders and staff, in just two days, reorientated their work to support pupils and families in lockdown during the Covid-19 pandemic. Under increasing economic pressure, "schools never gave up on helping. In families' hour of most desperate need … school leaders stepped in to make these things happen."

Emblematic of this work was the collective effort of many school leaders, professional associations, unions and charitable organisations to pressure the Department for Education into reversing its decision not to provide funding for free school meals during the Easter holidays of 2020. This was during the peak of the pandemic in the UK.

Funding is given to schools to provide free school meals (FSM) to disadvantaged children during term time. There is no funding for meals during school holidays, when children can often go hungry or fill up on low-cost meals of limited nutritional value. In the lead-up to the Easter holidays, I wrote the following blog post on behalf of Headteachers' Roundtable, sharing it using the hashtag #FSM4Easter:

OUR POOREST CHILDREN NEED HELP NOW

Over the past few weeks, schools – their governors, leaders, teachers and support staff – have risen to the civic challenge of helping our country face Covid-19. Among the many challenges of their essential work, ensuring children from the most disadvantaged families are adequately fed has been at the top of their agenda.

Yesterday [30 March], media sources were informed of the Department for Education's scheme for issuing free school meal (FSM) vouchers a full 11 hours before it was released to school. The embargo was until midnight on 30 March. The delay and timing of publication lacked common sense; it was not designed to support school leaders in meeting the needs of the nation's poorest children.

However, what has infuriated schools most is the Department for Education's decision not to fund FSM vouchers over the two-week Easter "break". This is despite the requirement for schools to be open but more importantly because children will go hungry. School budgets are already overstretched and no allowance has been made for these additional costs.

Official Department for Education figures (January 2019) show that there were just over 8.1 million children in maintained schools, of whom 1,247,409 were entitled to FSMs. The cost of funding every child with £30 to help feed them over the two weeks of Easter is circa £37.5 million.

At a time when hundreds of billions of pounds have rightly been used to support companies, employees and the self-employed, the figure is relatively small. For disadvantaged families, the impact of an additional £30 per child arriving immediately cannot be overstated. School governors and staff, working in the heart of their communities, know the additional impact of Covid-19 on families who for years have been struggling. We are in this together; we have to be in this together but especially for our most needy families, children and young people.

Please show your support by tweeting out about this campaign using the hashtag #FSM4Easter and contacting your local MP. We have 72 hours to make a difference.

A shortened version of the blog post appeared as a letter in *The Sunday Times* (5 April 2020). In addition, Sian Griffiths, the education and families editor of the paper, coordinated a piece campaigning for FSMs to be funded over Easter that involved Jamie Oliver, Bite Back 2030, School Food Matters and Headteachers' Roundtable. Then, at the Saturday afternoon government briefing on 4 April 2020, Michael Gove stood up to announce there would be a national FSM voucher system that included the period over the Easter holidays. This is the first time funding has ever been provided during the school holidays to families whose children are entitled to FSMs. I see it as a first step in bringing an end to holiday hunger.

Sadly, what followed was a bit of a debacle. The company running the scheme struggled with the demand placed on it, leading to exasperation among many overworked and stressed school leaders and business managers. A number of schools had already made the decision to fund FSMs over Easter themselves to ensure children didn't go hungry. The funding had come from their school budgets. Disappointingly, the Department for Education's refunding scheme meant these schools, having taken the highest ethical stance, were likely to be left out of pocket. All schools need to feed the hungry in their communities. Sometimes it's physical and at other times metaphorical.

Each school faces a set of challenges, often quite different depending upon context, when it comes to supporting the development of social capital within families and the local community. Citizenship is underpinned by a knowledge of issues and a sense of empowerment. It is about praxis – theory and action. However, knowing that I should love my neighbour is less of a challenge than actually loving them. The knowledge is not as powerful as the action.

I often liken my role as the leader of a Catholic school to that of a storyteller. This may be different for other headteachers. Some will be storytellers, but based in a different tradition, while others – in the absence of tradition, or owing to greater autonomy or the need to redefine the school's mission – will have to be storywriters as well as storytellers.

The storytelling element of a leader's role provides clarity to people about the essence or purpose of the school. Various shorthands will be used. For example, within a Catholic school we are called to be "priest, prophets and kings" to ensure that "God is known, truth is told and human needs are met". This describes the four dimensions of the pastoral mission of the church: kerygma (the proclaiming school), leitourgia (the worshipping school), diakonia (the serving school) and koinonia (the civic school). I had no autonomy in determining whether these were part of the mission of the schools I led. They were set. My autonomy was in how I brought them alive in the time and context of my leadership.

Kerygma and leitourgia give the distinctive roots to the school community. Diakonia and koinonia are the fruits, the concrete actions realised by all who see their schools at the heart of their community. Schools' desire to transform society, and to exist in reasonable harmony with and provide support to the surrounding community, is a hallmark of service and civic duty, emphasising social action in the service of the poor. Such schools see themselves as part of the network of relationships that stretch into the local community and its families.

Schools that prioritise preparation for citizenship will place an importance on the knowledge found in the local community. This is the embodied cultural capital that is formed by families and traditions from the constituent cultural groups. Such schools also have a genuine and deep-seated belief in ensuring representation from the local community, families and pupil body in the decision-making structures and processes within the school.

CHAPTER 9
What's your why?

Dylan Wiliam (2013) rightly talks about the "sometimes messy" compromise between the different philosophies of education. They can be seen as competing, either/or options: one philosophy may be given an overwhelming priority to the exclusion of others. Alternatively, the different philosophies of education may be seen as interlinking and mutually supportive elements.

> *"The important point about these four broad philosophies of education is that they are not alternatives from which we can choose our favourites. All are important, and often in tension with one another, and so any education system is a – sometimes messy – compromise between these four sets of aims."*
> Wiliam (2013)

Despite the value many place on oracy, it is largely pushed out of the curriculum in many schools. The chair of the Oracy All-Party Parliamentary Group, Emma Hardy MP, called for evidence to be submitted to the group's Speak for Change inquiry – part of a commitment to help "every child be a confident communicator and find their voice". As the current chair of Headteachers' Roundtable, I coordinated our response and submitted it in April 2019. It is an exploration of how the various different underpinning philosophies of education impact on education. These are the three main bullet points from our submission:

> *"Starting with the development of speech, language and communication in early years, through phonics, early reading and the acquisition of an extended vocabulary, oracy is an integral part of children developing the necessary literacy skills to be successful at school and beyond. This includes the development of disciplinary literacy that supports further academic and vocational studies and employment."*

"Children and young people must be given the opportunity and means to voice their thoughts, hopes, concerns and desires at a personal, community, national and international level. That is, they are empowered individually and collectively, within the democratic and societal processes, to bring purpose, direction and dignity to the lives of themselves and others. They need to be taught the skills. They have a right to be heard and the responsibility to exercise this right legally, responsibly and appropriately."

"Oracy is a fundamental life skill that enables young people to present, inform, discuss and converse with others. This helps them, for example, to succeed at interview – whether for paid employment, leading to high-quality apprenticeships or for a place at a prestigious university and in the workplace."

The submission highlighted the importance of cultural and disciplinary literacy, personal empowerment and social justice, and the use of oracy in the workplace. It brought alive how the different philosophies have a part to play in the overall education of children and young people.

In forming a view on the purpose of education, many factors come into play. These include the prevailing orthodoxy of the time, as well as previous experiences and deeply held beliefs. It is important to take care with claims about how a particular philosophy leads to a better education. Metrics like standardised assessment tests (SATs) will invariably conclude that cultural transmission and its associated curriculum create more effective schools. SATs may be an appropriate evaluative tool for measuring the accumulation of knowledge, but they are less appropriate if assessing social capital within families and the local community or personal empowerment.

In the current climate there is a danger that knowledge is seen as the next cure-all, the latest silver bullet. There is a danger of hyperbole, amplified through social media, that overstates its impact. Ten years on from promises of how the teaching of knowledge would close the inequalities gap in education, the attainment of the long-term disadvantaged has fallen slightly further behind their more affluent peers.

Concerns about claims made using Michael Young's work on powerful knowledge relate to the uniqueness of disciplinary knowledge as a discrete separate entity. Outside of aspects of mathematics and science, it is questionable to what extent some disciplinary knowledge is sufficiently different from everyday knowledge to warrant the claims that it is powerful (White, 2018).

The empirical evidence base for the curriculum as a solution to inequalities and school quality is incomplete.

> *"Where the Education Endowment Foundation has attempted to evaluate curriculum programmes (such as The Curriculum Centre's Word and World Reading Programme), the trials haven't signalled curriculum success (though this doesn't upset the wave, of course). And the centrepiece of the empirical evidence in ED Hirsch's book, a rough French data cross-tabulation, isn't particularly convincing to empiricists such as Christian Bokhove (or to us)."* Allen (2019)

Our system's current drive to place cultural transmission as the overriding philosophy of education will wane. Every action has an equal and opposite reaction. My hope is that the reaction will not be so extreme that we rebound to something else completely, forgetting the importance of knowledge. If I was writing this book a decade or more ago, I would be less concerned about whether we had in place drivers around personal empowerment and social cohesion, but rather would be bemoaning the lack of thought being given to the transmission of culture/knowledge. The lasting benefit of many people's current work is that when we are seeking to transmit culture/knowledge, we are more capable and skilled to do it effectively than we were previously.

Hirsch (1999) warns of the need to avoid the premature polarisation that arises when "educational policy is confused with political ideology". Examples of how people become hijacked into premature polarisation are manifold. Gove's "enemies of promise" comment in 2012 caused offence to many people. These people, rather than sitting in Westminster's ivory towers, had spent large parts of their careers teaching young people, including pupils from disadvantaged backgrounds. However, this shouldn't lead to a complete consequential rejection of the importance of knowledge or its organisation within subjects, exhibiting associated disciplinary knowledge. These established routes, particularly at GCSE and A-level, give pupils passports to higher levels of learning and in turn longer, happier and healthier lives on average.

Freire's framing of his ideas around personal empowerment in left-wing Marxist revolutionary language will grate with some. The underpinning concept of personal empowerment needs to be grasped, while the particular terminology can be parked or dropped. Inequalities in knowledge are not the only inequalities that young people and families from disadvantaged communities have to cope with. In some contexts, children and young people will arrive at school with a sense of personal empowerment and the family support that will enable them almost certainly to go on to further or higher education; others won't. Context mediates purpose. Schools often need to mitigate social factors.

Objections to the Gove/Gibb imposition of the English Baccalaureate, on 90% of young people, shouldn't lead to the wholesale rejection of a core curriculum or debating what it should be. Engaging in a thoughtful manner is important. For example, it allows you to question the latest inspection framework, as applied to primary schools. Subject-based deep dives (increasingly referred to as shallow paddles; a much more accurate descriptor) have a very particular curriculum view more aligned with disciplinary thinking than cultural literacy. A primary school may reasonably decide to place significantly less emphasis on organising the primary curriculum into subjects, but retain a focus on the cultural knowledge required to develop literacy.

Many primary schools' curriculums have often evolved in a thematic way focused on the development of literacy and its underpinning cultural knowledge. One person often teaches a range of subjects. Primary teachers are non-specialists in many of the areas in which they are required to teach. Professor Becky Allen (2019) expresses her concern that attempting to change this involves "disrupting a set of habits, beliefs, resources and practices". Reforming the primary foundation curriculum to a knowledge-rich, subject-based one is a significant challenge that may "make a stable, though very imperfect, curriculum into a highly unstable and chaotic one". Even if you accept that something might be a good idea in theory, it doesn't always mean it should be implemented in practice. Text without context can cause more problems than it solves – significant effort and heartache for no overall gain.

For some, power is associated with knowledge. Like many others, I could also talk about a lifetime of experience that has taught me the power of: the network or the community; the moment; good fortune; money; the confidence to act or to not act; working hard; sitting back; family and professional support; and a healthy disposition. In many situations and circumstances, knowledge was not the determining factor in moving my life forward. By way of balance, substantive and disciplinary knowledge provided me with qualifications to degree level that gave me access to teaching. Further, domain knowledge of education, as well as more generic knowledge associated with leadership, has helped me to have a rewarding career and the financial security that came with it. Aspects of empowerment, knowledge, beliefs and values, associated with people and communities, have all played a part.

When considering what you might believe the purpose of education to be, my suggestion is to follow a biblical process in your thinking. The Bible is organised in three main sections: the Law, the Prophets and Wisdom. In determining your overarching purpose of education, you are constructing the Law. It is a framework that will enable you to understand why you take certain approaches to the curriculum, pedagogy, pastoral care, behaviour and engagement with the community.

Your prophetic voice and that of others should use the alternative philosophies to critique your perspective. This allows you to challenge the framework you have established. Are your priorities coherent and clear? Are you happy with what is being omitted or given a lower priority, as well as with what you are seeing as important? To what extent does the coherence you are creating lead to a synergy between the constituent elements? Are there greater synergies that could be achieved? Finally, wisdom comes with the benefit of experience. The process is iterative.

The four philosophies of education are not mutually exclusive. They operate in tension, overlapping and competing for time and space. Neither knowledge nor personal empowerment are sufficient on their own to create a just and fair society. Education must seek to enhance both. This influenced the approaches I took as a teacher and school leader. Your purpose becomes enacted through a thousand different decisions and interactions. Purpose is where the reality of what is possible and desirable meet; orthopraxy trumps ideology.

THINK PIECE: WHAT'S YOUR PURPOSE?

Now that you have read the preceding chapters, what or who do you think should shape the education offered? Should education be moulded by and around the child or young person? Or to what extent should the child or young person be shaped by their education?

> *"What do we mean by 'education'? There are two Latin roots for the word: educare meaning to 'bring up, to train and to teach', and educere, meaning 'to lead and draw out that which lies within'. Together both meanings provide a helpful picture for what education should be."*   Sentamu (2016)

When considering the four key philosophies of education (Wiliam, 2013), what level of importance would you attach to each? Write a number from 0 to 5 next to each of the philosophies below: 0 would mean you think it is not relevant and important at all, while 5 would mean you believe it to be extremely relevant and important. These are not meant to be absolute measures, more a means by which to attach relative importance to the different philosophies.

1. To develop the potential of the child (personal empowerment).
2. To pass on "the best which has been thought and said" (cultural transmission).
3. To prepare young people for life and work (preparation for work).
4. To build communities and overcome social disadvantage (preparation for citizenship).

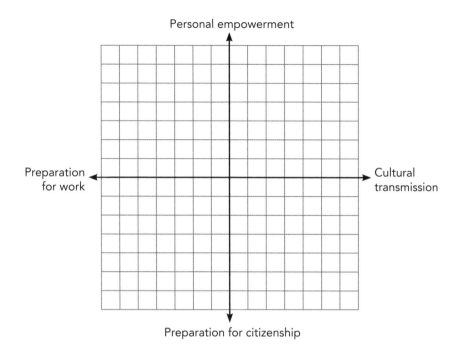

Personal empowerment

Preparation for work ← → Cultural transmission

Preparation for citizenship

Now, plot each of your four "scores" on the axis above and then join the four points. This will form a quadrilateral shape. The more regular the quadrilateral (the more it resembles a square), the greater the extent to which you place equal importance on the four philosophies when determining education's overall purpose. An irregular shape suggests that you give a greater priority to one, two or three of the underpinning philosophies.

There is no right or wrong answer. It is more about clarity of purpose and alignment when you act; choices have consequences. What are your thoughts or justification for the importance you attach to each of the philosophies? How are the different elements enacted in your school? Is your purpose a lived reality? What needs to change?

CHAPTER 10
Educating with purpose:
five different perspectives

This chapter presents a detailed exploration of the four underpinning philosophies of education from leaders in different school settings. Binks Neate-Evans provides an early years perspective. Sabrina Hobbs writes about purpose for a special school and Navdeep Sanghara writes from the perspective of primary schools. Ros McMullen offers her thoughts on purpose within secondary schools over time, while Dave Whitaker takes a view from alternative education. As you read, use these "prophetic voices" to challenge your current thinking.

Each of these five leaders has considered which of the philosophies of education they believe to be more or less important, plotting their scores on the axis. Their quadrilaterals are included alongside their words.

Binks Neate-Evans, executive principal, Evolution Academy Trust

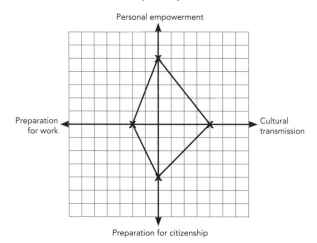

Personal empowerment

Preparation for work

Cultural transmission

Preparation for citizenship

The early years is arguably the most distinct phase of education. It sits outside of national curriculum requirements, with its own framework. I am slightly ashamed to say that I came to really understand and respect the critical value of early years relatively late in my career. Taking up my third headship in an infant and nursery school, in an urban area with very high levels of socioeconomic deprivation, honed my thinking and use of resource.

Leaders of infant schools know all too well that there is a very short window of opportunity to bring about improvement for children, particularly those who may have had impoverished early experiences. When considering the unique value of a particular stage or phase, ensuring that the right emphasis is placed at the right time for the right reasons is crucial. It's the how, why and when of modelling your school.

I still hang on to a few of my old teacher training books. I was privileged enough to train at time when the four-year BEd (Hons) was normal. This afforded me the luxury of one whole year of theory and philosophy of learning. My tutor was an unrelenting, unforgiving beast; she hammered away at our teaching files, ensuring that what we did was underpinned by theory.

The work of Ferre Laevers is highly influential in many early years settings. His aim is for the learning environment to enable children to be "like fish in water". The careful synchrony of adult interactions and an enabling environment manifest to create high levels of wellbeing and involvement for the child. Reflecting on Laevers' work, the internationally renowned early years specialist Jan Dubiel wrote:

> *"Building on the state of well-being is that of 'involvement', a deep cognitive 'immersion' in an activity and/or thinking. At these moments, multiple neurological connections take place, thinking is extended, and knowledge and skills are brought together to express an idea, solve a problem, communicate a thought, or achieve an action. Sometimes described as 'deep-level learning', it is the point at which learning is expressed in a powerful self-motivated way."* Dubiel (2014)

The first major European longitudinal study of a national sample of young children's development between the ages of three and seven demonstrated the intrinsic link between all four philosophies of education. It concluded:

> *" ... in most effective centres 'play' environments were used to provide the basis of instructive learning. However, the most effective pedagogy combines both 'teaching' and providing*

freely chosen yet potentially instructive play activities. Effective pedagogy for young children is less formal than for primary school but its curricular aims can be both academic as well as social and emotional." Sylva et al (2004)

Personal empowerment of the young learner is essential to provide the strong foundations that allow development of other aspects of learning in early years.

The tremendous and highly distinct rate of brain development in the early years is now more widely understood. Sir Robert Winston (2003) states that "the first two years are the most vital for language acquisition … the frequency with which parents speak to children up to the age of two has major consequences for their language use throughout the rest of their lives." These early experiences affect the architecture of the brain when it is at its most plastic. Emotional wellbeing and understanding of social interactions lay strong foundations for emerging cognitive development.

Children love complexity; ask a five-year-old to strip down an old washing machine or bike and watch. When cultural transmission is presented in the spirit of Jerome Bruner's "spiral curriculum", it has a powerful influence on education in the early years. It is where skilled practitioners/teachers build on young learners' curiosity and experiences with purposeful and thoughtful adult-directed learning: stories, rhymes, mathematical resourcing and games, alongside experiencing beauty, awe and wonder.

Without being able to integrate young learners into socially acceptable patterns of behaviour and learning, we would be doing them a disservice. They are young citizens. Preparedness for citizenship is equally as important as cultural transmission. Best practice in the early years helps children to manage their feelings, self-regulate and respect others. This helps them begin to understand more abstract concepts such as fairness, democracy and diversity. If education, even in the early years, doesn't help children to develop ideas of human decency, our world will become even more frightening as this becomes lost and undervalued. The skill is the balance between enhancing lived experiences and preparedness (not readiness) for the next stages of education.

Because of the powerful relationship between emotional/social development and cognitive development, the role and influence of early childhood experiences in schools and other settings is paramount. Achieving high-quality early years practice is incredibly complex and has been undervalued for years.

Childhood must be a valued stage in itself, not a means to an end. For this stage of education, preparation for work isn't as relevant. The caveat being that without a really strong foundation, we know children wobble through future learning, inevitably impacting on their familial economic health.

Neil Postman (1994), in his powerful account of the emergence and erosion of the social construct of childhood, writes: "It is not inconceivable that our culture will forget that it needs its children. But it's halfway to forgetting that children need childhood. Those who insist on remembering shall perform a noble service."

Sabrina Hobbs, principal, Severndale Specialist Academy, Shropshire

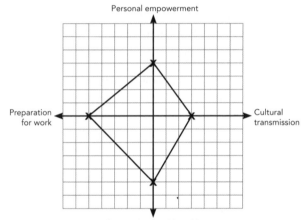

The purpose of education is a key question for all school leaders to reflect on from time to time, as different ideologies and systemic drivers can too often pull and push a school's ethos to the detriment of pupil-centred approaches and meaningful outcomes. This is even more pertinent in the specialist education sector, where many traditional strategies, curricula and "success" criteria for children/school leaders are irrelevant.

The pupils who attend specialist education are a broad and varied group. Cohorts include: pupils who have attended mainstream settings for a period of time and transitioned to a specialist setting; those who have extremely complex medical needs that impact on their physical, cognitive and sensory abilities; and those with severe autism and other learning difficulties that impact on social, emotional and communication skills. Other needs that impact on learning, which may or may not include a learning difficulty, are social, emotional and mental health (SEMH) difficulties, behavioural needs that are becoming more prevalent across specialist settings.

At Severndale Specialist Academy we cater for the full cross section of pupil need, from the ages of two to 25, across three different locations, for more than 450 children and young people. As expected, there will be distinctly different curriculums, resources and timetables to differentiate between the ages and SEND needs. However, the consistency comes from the overarching approach and ethos.

Reflecting on our special school ethos, the focus is heavily weighted towards community inclusion, where everyone is valued, everyone is included and everyone is learning (our school values). The emphasis is on "everyone". Not just pupils, but also staff, parents/carers, family members of staff and pupils, and the wider community of professionals, schools and neighbours. The reason? Because we are all responsible for shaping our next generation of adults, who will make society even better than it is today!

The reality for those with learning difficulties is that they rely heavily on the support of others. It is not something that they will ever grow out of, or that education or medical advances can eradicate over time. However, this does not mean that they want a handout. To the contrary, they want what most people want: a life with choices; to be accepted and wanted by others; a home to share with people who care; and to ultimately have a reason to get up in the morning (purpose).

With this in mind, we first identify tangible scenarios that would constitute a "successful" outcome for identified cohorts/individuals. For our most able pupils, a great outcome would include paid employment/voluntary-sector work, moving into appropriate semi-independent living, and having healthy hobbies and a social life that is safe and secure. For our least able pupils, we hope that their adulthood is one where they are able to anticipate the routines of life and positively participate, have fun with people, know how best to communicate basic needs, and be able to utilise coping strategies to manage their anxieties and frustrations.

On first glance, this seems simple. However, an issue arises if we only see our academic/vocational offer in isolation. No matter how "life-ready and prepared" our pupils are, their family, current/future communities, current/ future employers and current/future leaders (including doctors, social workers and MPs) won't be, unless we prepare and teach them, too.

Where are our future "supporters" in the community, future employers and future leaders right now? Right now, they are children in mainstream schools, both in the private and maintained sectors. Unless we make a concerted effort to integrate mainstream and specialist provisions, those mainstream children will grow up never knowing how to support or make a difference to those with learning difficulties, as they will never have learned the value of including everyone. As Gandhi said, "The future depends on what you do today." Therefore, inclusion becomes more of a necessity, rather than a choice, in what we need to do to shape a better, more inclusive society for those with learning difficulties.

Reflecting back to the four philosophies of education, this is the rationale for the identification of preparation for life and work and building communities and overcoming disadvantage as equally the most important aspects of our educational ethos. Developing potential (personal empowerment) is likely to be an important feature to any school, as we maximise life chances by identifying individual strengths and abilities. However, the functionality of this aspect dictates the level of success. A child with severe autism may be gifted in maths but unable to cope well with social interactions, presenting high levels of anxiety with violent, unpredictable outbursts. Concentrating on this potential for maths would not enable the child to achieve the outcomes for a successful life. However, by overcoming those barriers and developing this strength, we will certainly build confidence, character and a skill set to offer and contribute if honed.

Cultural transmission, to pass on knowledge, may be the least important aspect for our SEND pupils; however, it is still important. Cultural capital creates interest, understanding and opens up opportunities to talk to someone. A minority of people with learning difficulties get jobs or are active participants in our current societal model. Unfortunately, of that minority, the majority struggle most with "appropriateness" of conversation and social etiquette. Passing on "the best which has been thought and said" gives some structure and context on which our pupils can build, as they practise their skills during inclusion activities, and then utilise them later in life while chatting to colleagues on their lunch break or helping customers in the workplace. In conclusion, all four philosophies of educational purpose play a part in our specialist settings in order to achieve successful outcomes for all our pupils.

Navdeep Sanghara, executive headteacher, Inspire Partnership, London

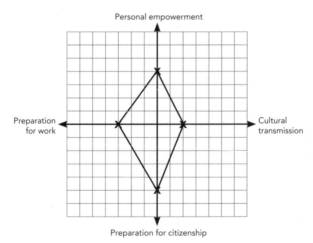

Schools connect communities to create another community and, although they prepare children and young people for examinations and the world of work, they are so much more than that. If the global pandemic has provided us with any lessons learned, it would be that although we can use websites to upload home learning and YouTube to stream virtual assemblies, without physical interaction, without our children (and their families), it feels soulless and lacks meaning.

> *"Education is not the filling of a pail, but the lighting of a fire."*
> William Butler Yeats

Children enter our early years settings having already experienced such diversity in their start to life, some with rich connections both with their families and their neural pathways, others not. Given such disparity, it is our moral duty to develop children as individuals who have the confidence to meet the world and change it. Empowering children to think critically, learn and reflect is an integral purpose of primary education. Helping children to learn to be learners, build relationships, engage in dialogue and develop character will ultimately enable them to feel confident and empowered to contribute to society in a way which has meaning to them.

Therefore, the curriculum on offer for every child should centre on quality and depth, providing children with the knowledge alongside opportunities to practise and apply this in meaningful ways, where they interact with their learning rather than being receivers of it. The impact is powerful, leading to more socially aware, confident, reflective learners.

A definition of cultural transmission that concentrates solely on knowledge acquisition and intellect is a narrow one. Although it is undeniable that knowledge acquisition is an integral part of education, the concept of "the best which has been thought and said" is more complicated.

In the years during which primary education was based on the National Strategies and ready-to-roll-out schemes, educational values deteriorated. Pupils became products, with teaching viewed as the transference of information from one vehicle to another. The measurement of testing was valued more than deep experiences of learning. The current Ofsted framework continues to be problematic in this respect; there is a need to be cautious that "knowing more and remembering more" does not become a value judgement about an individual (or a school). The purpose of education is far more than that.

Who defines and decides what "the best" of anything is? The importance of curriculum design becomes absolutely crucial here, as does the need for leaders to truly lead learning – to design and offer children a rich curriculum that is underpinned by cultural values, diversity and ethics.

If we consider this philosophy in relation to Bloom's domains of learning, then it simply does not take into account the affective domain: that an individual can only truly engage with something when they love it. This goes beyond acquiring knowledge and means deeply feeling it and using it to create something new.

Educated workers are more productive and the impact of this is felt economically. However, preparation for work depends on how we choose to view what "being educated" is. Schools need to be viewed as more than exam factories. In recent years, the global community has recognised that the relationship between educational success and soft skills is equally as important as the more formal skills and knowledge gained from a quality education. The publication of the PwC report *Navigating the Rising Tide of Uncertainty* (2020) highlights concerns about the availability of skills such as critical thinking, creativity and teamwork as the key to long-term success.

No one would dispute that we want to prepare our children to meet the world and find their place in it, but with the traditional routes of formal education and university degrees no longer fully reflecting the contemporary working world, education needs to go beyond just preparation for work. We need to ensure that our education system sees its purpose as providing children with opportunities to respect and consider the views of others, to develop a moral compass and to care for others.

> *"Bringing people together is what I call 'ubuntu' – I am because we are."* Desmond Tutu

Peter Block (2008) summarises, "A learning community's wellbeing has a lot to do with the quality of relationships, cohesion, inter-dependence and belonging." Schools are communities, best placed to embody the values required of an increasingly complex society.

Teachers delivering food parcels, phoning and texting families, conveying messages of love and hope via TikTok, and the hundreds of other creative acts by schools during lockdown further strengthen the idea that the education system and schools are in a unique position to serve and empower communities. The purpose of education has to be driven by a desire to provide children with not only the knowledge they need but also the skills to take this knowledge, make sense of it, question it and translate it into an action that is for the greater good.

In an era with widening gaps between the haves and have-nots, stronger tribal identities emerging through the polarisation of political parties and ideologies, and a risk of living in echo chambers, the purpose of education must inherently focus on the development of social capital within families and the community.

Education has a moral and social duty to ensure students find their place in the world, contribute more effectively and connect people together. Barack Obama, in his virtual commencement address at a ceremony for graduates of historically black colleges and universities in May 2020, said: "... so much of your generation has woken up to the fact that the status quo needs fixing; that the old ways of doing things don't work; and that it doesn't matter how much money you make if everyone around you is hungry and sick; that our society and democracy only works when we think not just about ourselves, but about each other."

Only by placing community and the enhancement of collective social capital at the heart of our work will we raise standards for all children. The purpose of education debate is multifaceted, but at the core we need an ethical, relational approach to leading which continuously reflects on what we do and why we do it. Our principles need to be guided by what we deeply value for the long-term benefit of our communities.

Ros McMullen, recently retired after years of headship and executive headship in secondary schools in disadvantaged communities

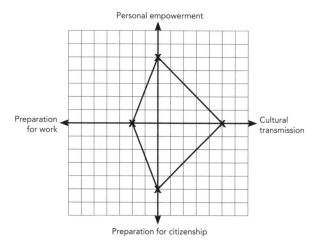

The various contexts within which I have served have always determined where I would place the different philosophies of education in the overall purpose. At the beginning of my leadership journey, my passion for social justice would have had me ranking preparation for citizenship, closely followed by personal empowerment, as the main philosophies of education that drove my vision. Looking back on how I prioritised school improvement in the early

1990s, I was closely focused on the culture of the school and particularly what was known as "the hidden curriculum". Working as a deputy head in a boys' secondary modern, I saw that one of the most significant factors in any child's achievements was what they believed to be true about their own potential. Consequently, I set about adjusting the experience of school to be one which focused on creating a circle of positivity around each child: extra-curricular experiences, pastoral support and opportunities for success in "citizenship activities" were central to all the initiatives I developed.

My first headship, at the turn of the century, was in a school serving a community where unemployment and worklessness had been an issue for several generations. In this context, I saw the main purpose of school improvement as ensuring that the generation I was educating would be the first generation of economically active adults: preparation for work became the primary focus of all initiatives. I did not chase a climb up the performance league tables, but instead developed a curriculum that ensured student destinations in the local economy. We introduced NVQ qualifications, in partnership with local employers, so that KS4 students all spent at least one full day in the world of work. What we found was that this experience motivated the students to achieve their maths and English GCSEs because their "employers" told them this was important. I employed tradesman to deliver practical subjects within the school and had many arguments with the local authority about paying them proper salaries.

The culture of the school and the messages to students and parents were all about the world of work and the importance of employment. The biggest food factory in Europe was on our doorstep; senior managers from there joined the governing body and provided practical interview experience for students, together with helping to devise the careers curriculum. We became a specialist Business and Enterprise College and student attendance rose dramatically, as did GCSE results. It was an area of extreme deprivation and there was an agreement between all professionals working in the area that tackling worklessness was the way to reduce crime, improve health and eradicate poverty. At this stage in my leadership journey, preparation for work and preparation for citizenship were combined to give purpose to the education we offered.

When I moved from this headship to open one of the first academies, I was initially focused in a very similar way, but the political context began to change, with a much greater pressure on schools to concentrate on "academic" outputs. As we moved through the early 2000s, I also began to notice that although we could become relatively successful in "getting kids through exams", these young people would often struggle when moving on to the next academic stage, as we were too focused on merely hitting the output targets set for us. In particular, the students we sent off to universities often dropped out. We began to focus more on the how and the what we delivered in the curriculum: our students needed to have some of the "spoon-feeding" and "scaffolding" removed, and they needed a richer curriculum which would develop a passion for learning for its own sake. One of the key initiatives we undertook was to become an International Baccalaureate World School. In our context, this was easier than it is for most, as the parents were not fixated on A-levels, having had no experience of them or of higher education personally. Preparation for work was not a key purpose of education in our context at this time: unemployment was far less of an issue than low pay and black economy work. Our challenge was cultural transmission.

In my last few years of leading a number of secondary academies, I have become far more focused on cultural transmission as the main philosophy of education, seeing it as essential in the quest for social justice. The curriculum is the key product and the one thing we can control and adjust for our context. It also enables us to shape the structures and the budget in the most appropriate way to effect school improvement. I now believe that a failure to give students "the best which has been thought and said" deprives them of an ability to flourish in the modern world and has to be the key focus of the school. Having a clear vision for cultural transmission enables us to address the other philosophies of education. I don't think the young Ros had it wrong 20 years ago by concentrating on preparation for work – that was right in that context. It wouldn't be central to my thinking in current times.

Dave Whitaker, director of learning, Wellspring Academy Trust, South Yorkshire

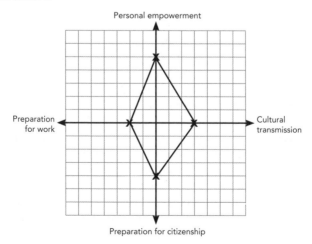

Having spent years working with vulnerable children who struggle on a day-to-day basis to conform, I believe it is important to reflect on leadership priorities and the focus for a school's values and ethos. I often reflect on the "leadership journey" and whether priorities change or are influenced by policy or "the system". Ultimately, priorities change as you experience and recognise their impact on your school community, rather than because someone tells you what you should prioritise. This is confident and brave leadership. In a SEMH setting, the children are very often from seriously challenging environments. Many have been exposed to adverse childhood experiences, social exclusion and deprivation. When this is prevalent in a school, then the focus and direction of that establishment must respond. It is the responsibility and the duty of the school, and its leadership, to respond to what it sees as the priority – irrespective of what judgements others may make and associate with success.

Personal empowerment sits proudly as the highest priority. Children in alternative provision, often excluded from school and from society, lack self-esteem and confidence. They struggle to make emotional connections or to trust adults, and often survive in a constant state of high arousal. Their challenging behaviours can be a response to this and not a choice they make – neuroscience tells us such. They do not believe in themselves, have low aspirations and do not trust the world around them. As leaders, acceptance of this is a priority. Everyone needs to feel part of something and children in alternative provision and SEMH settings will struggle to feel part of school unless the school itself makes this happen. Without being understood, the children will not build self-esteem and in turn will not be confident. As a leader, I have always been mindful of "conformity" and its potential to restrict personal growth. Do we need to change their culture to suit ours, or should we empower them to be proud and confident in who they are?

Preparation for citizenship can never be ignored in schools where there is an obvious deficit in social capital, communities are struggling and families feel ignored and misunderstood. Building confidence in young people who lack aspiration starts in the classrooms and corridors of school. The responsibility lies in every interaction that young person has with both adults and peers. There is also a collective responsibility from wider stakeholders. Here lies another problem, as access to wider support, third-party organisations and additional funding is varied. In London and other metropolitan areas, the charitable sector is prevalent and prolific. The impact of their work is high as they support families, work in partnership with schools and provide sustainable, additional support that schools cannot resource. However, there is a widening gap of disadvantage for those schools in smaller, often highly deprived towns and rural areas. In these scenarios, the school carries the whole burden, additional support is limited and resources are stretched. Building social capital rests on the shoulders of the school and therefore raises its priority and importance to society.

Cultural transmission, as important as it is, cannot sit higher in the priorities than those previously discussed. However, if we can generate curiosity in our pupils, then they are more likely to develop an emotional attachment to their teachers and therefore behave appropriately and learn more. A priority for me has always been to create interest from pupils in the curriculum. In fact, I use the quality of teaching as the cornerstone of behaviour policy, even in a SEMH or AP setting.

Preparation for work is clearly a significant issue for children who have fallen out of mainstream provision and those with academic deficits. However, if we get the other priorities right then this will automatically be addressed. Children with SEMH difficulties are often talented and hard-working, yet they can struggle to manage their emotions and conform to expectations and standards without support. That said, preparation for work may come more easily in an AP setting, as a more vocational curriculum can allow children to access the workplace developmentally and over a longer period – preparation for work is embedded in the curriculum. Children can thrive in AP when a school skilfully develops an appropriate work-related offer for its pupils. Also, where personal empowerment and preparation for citizenship have been a priority of the school, children are better prepared for their next steps and the transition to work. It is the natural order or hierarchy within the schools to allow successful preparation for work to be a result of other key priorities.

CHAPTER 11
Purpose enacted: the curriculum

Discussions and disagreements about curriculum are often a proxy for discussions and disagreements about the purpose of education. While the underpinning philosophies are distinct, they are not mutually exclusive and may best be considered as a series of overlapping circles. They hold in tension a school's or a person's overall view of the purpose of education. Dylan Wiliam believes that simplistic choices are unhelpful:

> *"Rather than 'either/or' thinking we need 'both/and' thinking. The curriculum should be child-centred and subject-centred (and society-centred too). It should regard emotional development and intellectual development not as alternatives but as strands in a rope, which mutually strengthen each other. The curriculum has to take into account the needs of individuals and society while at the same time being sensitive to local constraints and affordances."* Wiliam (2013)

He concludes that this level of complexity means "there can never be a satisfactory step-by-step model for curriculum development – the problem is just too complex to be solved with a recipe". Instead, Wiliam produced seven curriculum design principles. Their purpose is evaluative and they can be used to determine what is prioritised and what is not in any particular curriculum plan.

Professor Becky Allen, working with Ben White, expands on this issue of complexity when discussing the "wicked problem" of school improvement:

> *"A complex system cannot ever be understood in terms of deterministic mechanisms and pathways. Complexity is better thought of [as] an intractable knot that nobody can undo, even if they work on it for a lifetime. The best we can hope for is to*

make it sit a little better. This is why the problems of complex systems – such as making schools better or closing inequalities in attainment – are often called wicked problems." Allen (2019)

The curriculum is one such wicked problem. A curriculum breathes life into a school's or a teacher's beliefs about education. It is purpose enacted. The different philosophies of education place different emphases on aspects of curriculum design.

Wiliam's design principles (2013) can shape thinking, discussion and, in time, determination about what curriculum will be implemented. Alignment between the purpose of education, curriculum design and enactment is crucial. Discussion of the curriculum should be inexorable in schools.

The principles can be used as the basis of a shared vocabulary around curriculum. For some, one principle may predominate and as a consequence a particular curriculum and pedagogy will be implemented.

Dylan Wiliam's curriculum design principles

Balanced	Promotes intellectual, moral, spiritual, aesthetic, creative, emotional and physical development as equally important.
Rigorous	Seeks to develop intra-disciplinary habits of mind; the subject matter is taught in a way that is faithful to its discipline.
Coherent	Makes explicit connections and links between the different subjects/experiences encountered.
Vertically integrated	Focuses on progression by carefully sequencing knowledge; provides clarity about what "getting better" at the subject means.
Appropriate	Seeks to avoid making unreasonable demands by matching level of challenge to a pupil's current level of maturity/knowledge.
Focused	Looks to keep the curriculum manageable by teaching the most important knowledge; identifies the big ideas or key concepts within a subject.
Relevant	Seeks to connect the valued outcomes of a curriculum to the pupils being taught it; provides opportunities for pupils to make informed choices.

Next, I will explore the potential implications of the various philosophies of education on the curriculum principles that might be prioritised. It's important to note that it is not just the principles that change but also the knowledge that forms the content of the curriculum. The extent to which knowledge leads to action (praxis) varies.

Cultural transmission

In a school where the main purpose of education is cultural transmission, through the teaching of subjects, the key principles used to design the curriculum are likely to be rigour and vertical integration. These principles are required because of the specialised disciplinary knowledge being covered.

A rigorous curriculum is designed to develop intra-disciplinary habits of mind. The subject matter is taught in a way that is faithful to the discipline from which it is drawn. Michael Young provides examples of how different subjects enable different powerful ways to move from particular examples or contexts towards generalisations:

> " ... the sciences generate the power of abstraction and generalization; the social sciences provide weaker sources of generalisation, but they also provide new ways of imagining how people and institutions behave. The humanities do not provide the bases for generalization but they can show ... how the particular, a character for example in a great play or story, can represent something about humanity in general."
>
> Young (2014)

These are the disciplinary habits of mind that form a critical component of a rigorous curriculum.

Wiliam (2013) uses the example of heat transfer (as opposed to cold transfer) to explain how a physicist thinks: "For example, on a cold day, most people would explain their perception of the effect of the wind as being caused by the cold wind coming through their clothes, while anyone who has been trained as a physicist would explain this as heat being carried away from the body."

To see cold as an entity, rather than understand it as an absence of heat, would undermine understanding about energy transfer. Similarly, the everyday notion, sometimes promoted in news bulletins, that we are running out of energy would be rejected by scientists. The law of conservation of energy brings a different perspective. Energy can neither be created nor destroyed; energy can be transferred or changed from one form to another. We have enough energy, just not in a form that we find most useful. These disciplinary habits of mind are incorporated into the subjects that constitute the curriculum and become the building blocks of pupils' daily experiences.

A vertically integrated curriculum is designed for progression. Within subject areas, knowledge is carefully sequenced. New knowledge builds on what was taught earlier, with each stage a prerequisite for future learning. There is clarity about what improves when someone "gets better" at the subject.

In teaching any body of knowledge there is a need to be selective; you cannot teach everything. There is a requirement to ensure that the knowledge taught is sufficient and sufficiently connected to enable pupils to develop a coherent conceptual understanding of the subject.

> *"In devising curricular progressions, it is important to realise that very few curricular sequences are universal, even in a subject as linear as mathematics ... In other less linear subjects, there is even greater freedom for us to teach things in the sequence that makes most sense. I do not mean to suggest that 'anything goes'. Rather teachers have both considerable freedom, and considerable responsibility, to sequence the curriculum."*   Wiliam (2013)

The questions that teachers may discuss when planning schemes of learning or longer-term plans might include:

- Which aspect of our subject do we most need pupils to learn? Why? How do we know/what evidence do we have that this would lead to a greater understanding (higher quality of education) for pupils?
- As time is finite, what will we *not* teach? What impact will this have on the overall narrative within our subject?
- What is the most sensible order in which to teach these concepts to aid pupils' understanding? How will we sequence and connect the individual elements/aspects of knowledge to aid schema development? How critical is the order determined?

This leads to the sequencing of individual pieces of knowledge (facts) to form ideas and the connecting of these ideas to form overarching concepts. Planning requires significant thought, aided by experience, as to what should be taught and in what order. This is often termed as curricular progression or learning flow.

It is worth noting that if the curriculum was focused on cultural literacy (Hirsch, 1988) then either a subject or a thematic curriculum approach would be reasonable. The principles would be different for a thematic curriculum. This is based upon coherence (horizontal alignment) with the more middle-level, general understanding that can be the focus of the primary school curriculum. As ever, the exact purpose has an impact on the principles that are prioritised.

Personal empowerment

In a school where the primary purpose of education is personal empowerment, the key principle drivers of the curriculum are likely to be relevance, balance and coherence.

A relevant curriculum seeks to connect outcomes to the pupils being taught. It provides opportunities for pupils to make informed choices. For a young child, making informed decisions about how they learn is an important part of the development of their executive functioning. This is linked to later metacognitive skills and self-regulation.

I find early years classrooms fascinating places, but also quite an alien culture. To the uninformed, they may look like a free-for-all. The expert early years practitioner has provided a whole series of activities to choose from. The children can't just do anything they like. Rather, they can choose between activities carefully designed to: develop them physically – both gross and fine motor skills; develop their speech, language and communication skills; develop their literacy and numeracy; develop them socially, emotionally and creatively; and enhance their understanding of the world. When required, help is given to the children to support good choices.

For older pupils, opportunities to make informed choices about which aspects of the curriculum are of greatest interest, match their aptitude(s) or most suit their future career direction tend to be given a high priority. There tends to be a smaller core curriculum to allow for these choices to be made.

In developing the whole child, with the aim of personal empowerment, there is a need for a balanced curriculum. That is, one that promotes intellectual, moral, spiritual, aesthetic, creative, emotional and physical development as equally important. This is different to cultural transmission, which would prioritise the intellectual development of the child.

A broad and balanced curriculum allows children to experience success in areas where they may have a liking or leaning. It also requires them to experience different aspects of a balanced education, to ensure that they are not limited by their own circumstances or current preferences. This is particularly important for those from disadvantaged backgrounds. Unhelpfully, in many of the most economically and geographically isolated areas, access to cultural opportunities is more limited.

Ofsted's published inspection handbook (2019) states that pupils must be "able to access a broad and balanced curriculum at key stage 2. In secondary education, inspectors will expect to see a broad, rich curriculum." A "broad" curriculum consists of a range of subjects. "Rich" is an ill-defined term when it comes to enactment. There is no expectation of a balanced curriculum in key stage 3.

This is no accident or simple omission. In the joint Headteachers' Roundtable and Worth Less? response to Ofsted's draft inspection framework, we pointed out: "Whilst the inspection handbook refers to a broad curriculum or broad range of subjects on nine separate occasions, only once does it refer to a balanced curriculum." The one reference to "balanced" at key stage 3 disappeared.

Alongside the emphasis on the English Baccalaureate within the Ofsted framework, it seems clear that the intellect must be the overriding priority of the new framework. The moral, spiritual, aesthetic, creative, emotional and physical development of children is a lesser priority. This isn't a simple argument about right or wrong. My views on this are not neutral – they are formed and informed through decades of working in some of the most deprived communities in England. Rather, this is about what you believe education is for and whether the ever-changing imposition of Ofsted's beliefs on all schools is reasonable. It's also worth noting that the final inspection handbook doesn't refer to a balanced curriculum in key stage 1 either.

In order to enhance the personal empowerment of each child, there is a need to develop individual talents, including those that might be latent. For this reason, the maintenance of the creative and aesthetic arts alongside the personal, social and emotional development of the child is viewed as an important integral part of the curriculum. It is not an add-on, nor would it be considered the domain of parents as opposed to schools.

It's worth noting that there can be a tension between balanced and relevant when moving from principles into policy and practice. I explain more below. Tensions do not only exist between principles owing to the different philosophies of education, but can also exist between the principles emphasising a particular philosophy.

A coherent curriculum makes explicit connections and links between the different subjects/experiences encountered. This tends to lead to a curriculum that is more thematic in organisation than one based on subjects. It allows for teaching around real-world problems that are often multidisciplinary in nature.

The primary curriculum often has a greater coherence than the secondary one. The predominantly one-teacher-per-class structure lends itself to making links across subjects. This thematic curriculum can also support reading for understanding/comprehension. Teacher pedagogies are likely to transfer – for example, strategies to increase word depth and breadth and pre-teaching vocabulary are more likely to be prevalent during the teaching of a range of subjects. However, from a subject perspective, history may not be taught chronologically and science or geography may be taught as isolated topics, lacking an underpinning conceptual framework. Rigour (habits of minds; ways of thinking within disciplines) is given a lower priority.

Coherence, with its focus on aligning learning across subjects/the curriculum, can also disrupt vertical integration (sequencing and progress within a subject). As links between different subjects across the curriculum are made, they tend to distort or disrupt learning progressions within the subjects.

At a secondary level, we often see the reverse: greater vertical integration and rigour, but limited or no discussion between departments to create coherence across subjects. There isn't necessarily a right or a wrong; there just needs to be an acceptance that priorities have consequences. Schools must think through what they believe and value and then how best to implement it.

From principles to policy and practice

While I was CEO of the Blessed Edward Bamber Catholic Multi Academy Trust (a mixed-phase trust of one 11-18 secondary school and two one-form-entry primaries), our beliefs about why we educate were encapsulated in the curriculum, teaching, assessment and learning policy, largely written in the 2014/15 academic year and updated in 2019. A set of curriculum statements within the policy were descriptions of the curriculum at its best:

1. *"The curriculum will be broad, balanced and appropriate."*
2. *"The curriculum will be vertically integrated, to ensure progression, and focused on the big ideas and concepts that underpin subject understanding or development within the phase."*
3. *"The curriculum will be coherent within early years; becoming increasingly rigorous as pupils progress from key stage 1 to 5."*

In point 3, the term "rigorous" is used in the disciplinary sense, referring to the different habits of mind that govern how scientists, historians, linguists, mathematicians, artists and musicians approach their subject. Our work in the early years tended towards a more thematic, cross-disciplinary approach. This was most true in communication and literacy but less prevalent in mathematics. As pupils moved through the age ranges, the thematic curriculum became more subject-based and rigorous.

In our policy, each main statement had a series of sub-statements that gave more detail as to how the principles were to be implemented across the trust. Due to the cross-phase nature of the trust, and leadership lessons learned over time about the inappropriateness of being overly prescriptive, we sought to create an overarching policy framework but not a straitjacket. The implementation of these sub-statements, described below, exposes the inherent tensions that exist.

For point 1, "The curriculum will be broad, balanced and appropriate", the sub-statements were:

- *"A balanced curriculum – promoting intellectual, moral, spiritual, aesthetic, creative, emotional and physical development – will be available to all pupils within the trust, covering a broad range of subjects and experiences."*
- *"Teachers using their professional expertise and experience to set high expectations and challenge whilst ensuring curriculum content is in the zone of proximal development for pupils."*
- *"The systematic development of literacy, in particular reading and vocabulary acquisition and understanding across all key stages."*
- *"Year 9 pupils will be allowed limited choice within disciplines; maintaining a broad academic core of study – studying fewer subjects in greater depth – and balanced curriculum."*
- *"At key stages 4 and 5, allowing increased relevance through pupils' informed choices that allow for a greater depth of study with more limited breadth and balance."*

The curriculum changed as pupils moved from early years to sixth form; requiring a "balanced" curriculum to be available to all pupils is not the same as saying all pupils will study one. Although pupils didn't start their GCSEs in Year 9, we allowed some limited choice. Balance was maintained through the core curriculum (English, mathematics, science, RE, MFL, PE and PSHE) and the limited "options" were organised so that the choices were between subjects *within* a discipline, rather than allowing pupils to opt out of a particular discipline. This is part of empowering young people. They made informed choices.

At key stage 4, a balanced curriculum was available to all pupils but some chose, for reasons of personal preference or future career aspirations, to opt for a particular set of subjects. This could result in the loss of one or more elements of a balanced curriculum. As the core curriculum has always been relatively large at key stage 4, I was more than happy for young people to make an informed choice about one or two options. That is, to have a more relevant curriculum even if an aspect of balance was lost. Other school leaders and teachers may not be happy with that. Nowadays, in most schools, I'd guess that six or seven subjects are mandated, with pupils having a more open choice of only one or two GCSEs.

Similarly, at A-level (key stage 5), a student may opt for a particular programme of study that is largely intellectual, with limited or no aesthetic or creative elements. We used to insist that post-16 students followed a general studies programme, for all its faults, to help maintain balance. That option is no longer available.

Preparation for work

Similar to personal empowerment, relevance is a dominant principle in a school where preparation for work is the main purpose of education. However, relevance within this particular philosophy of education is primarily connected to choices about future career direction. The juxtaposition between a more work-orientated, project-based curriculum and its underpinning substantive and disciplinary knowledge creates an interesting interplay between a vertically integrated curriculum – to an extent, one that is rigorous – and coherence. Engineering is rooted in science and mathematics, with their convergent approach to knowledge. They seek to produce overarching laws and theories. However, engineering is also governed by the far more divergent thinking associated with design technology. Its purpose is to create practical, not theoretical solutions. The curriculum requires a series of interesting compromises.

In University Technical Colleges there is often an academic core consisting of English, mathematics and sciences (biology, chemistry and physics). Computer studies, business studies and engineering often appear as part of a specialist core. When well taught, these will be vertically integrated and ensure that key academic principles pertinent to the subject are learned. However, the emphasis is not purely on the discipline. There is also a focus on developing links to application. The knowledge taught must be functional and transferable outside of the discipline in which it was taught. To an extent, the disciplinary habits of mind (rigour) are less prominent. This is sometimes reflected by the use of vocational/occupational or industry-standard qualifications.

Although other subjects might be available as options – humanities, modern foreign languages and aesthetic subjects – these are not mandated. There is the potential for the curriculum offered to be balanced, but the different dimensions are not considered of equal importance in a curricular sense.

Significant space is required in the curriculum for the development of more workplace-orientated projects and approaches. These employability skills would include industrial/commercial problem-solving approaches that require: self- and project-management skills; teamwork, collaboration and leadership; enquiry and analysis; and creativity or innovation. Close links with industry or a particular sponsoring company allow for work placements that again emphasise the application of knowledge outside of the academic discipline. A curriculum associated with employability skills will be more coherent, requiring knowledge from a range of curriculum subjects and approaches that are not subject-bound.

One of the challenges within the current centrally proposed curriculum model, at key stage 4, is how this particular philosophy of education may be manifest in most maintained schools or academies. I'd suggest that within just about every school or academy, there are young people who would wish to give and would benefit from their curriculum having far greater work-placed relevance. Current insistence on the English Baccalaureate is a significant barrier. Requiring those pupils to transfer to University Technical Colleges at 14 isn't always possible or desirable.

Preparation for citizenship

There is a connection between personal empowerment and preparation for citizenship: "The pursuit of full humanity, however, cannot be carried out in isolation or individualism, but only in fellowship and solidarity" (Freire, 2017). Consequently, in terms of the key curriculum principles, relevance, coherence and balance all feature. However, within each of the principles there is a difference in enactment – a move of perspective from the individual to the community; from the "I" to the "we".

As such, relevance is no longer tied to individual interests and aspirations, but aligned with what is of importance to the wider community. Aspects of local and familial culture and the impact of current issues on this culture become key aspects of the curriculum. In part, there is a need for a more coherent curriculum that cuts across disciplinary boundaries, whereas other aspects like music, dance and faith can sit within a more subject-based curriculum. This begins to answer the question of whether Mozart or Stormzy, da Vinci or Banksy should be on the curriculum. Both Stormzy and Banksy could be utilised to challenge some of the prevailing orthodoxy, while their works could be challenged themselves for some of their content. Their relevance is due to their commentary on society as it is currently perceived.

The curriculum, in its widest sense, would include projects and programmes that would lead to direct work with and within local communities. The intellectual, moral, spiritual, aesthetic, creative, emotional and physical developments of a balanced curriculum could be articulated and developed within the classroom, but would also need to be part of a programme of social action in the community. A number of "employability skills" would be seen as important in developing young people's work within the community. Links with local and community groups would be deep and long-term.

All the above philosophies have implications beyond the curriculum. They impact on every aspect of a school's life and what is valued. For example, a term like "engagement" would be seen very differently depending on the school's perspective. From a cultural transmission perspective, Professor Robert Coe (2013) suggests that "learning happens when people have to think hard". Although he adds that this definition "is over-simplistic, vague and not original", it allows us to move beyond proxies of learning to how pupils engage in learning. From an intellectual perspective, engagement in learning involves pupils thinking hard about that which they should be thinking hard about.

However, if viewed through the lens of preparation for citizenship, engagement is more likely to refer to an element of praxis – involvement and commitment to projects that promote or enhance community cohesion or empowerment. Neither is good or bad per se. There is a need to align the curriculum, pastoral care and aspects of culture to the overarching purpose and the influence of the different educational philosophies.

Narrowing the curriculum or shallowing the curriculum?

"Curriculum narrowing" is frequently used within education circles as a pejorative term. What is less prevalent is the counterbalance within the debate: shallowing the curriculum. As with many tensions that exist in the curriculum, breadth and depth are a deadly embrace. More of one inevitably leads to less of the other; time is finite.

At extremes, would you prefer your curriculum to be a mile wide and an inch deep, or an inch wide and a mile deep? Most of us are likely to prefer neither, but rather something in between. However, once you get off the theoretical fence and actually implement a curriculum, there are decisions to be made. Developing a curriculum for a school, key stage or subject requires a whole series of choices about what to include and in what order, as well as the much more challenging decision of what to omit. Curriculum planning at a whole-school and departmental/phase level is all about priorities. Should English and mathematics receive more time in the curriculum than art, drama and music (sometimes added together) or more than history, geography or religious studies? How much more? This decision has significant consequences for what can be covered in these other subjects, in their more limited or expansive time allowance.

In the key stage 3 curriculum, breadth requires the coverage of a large number of foundation subjects in a limited amount of time. Many foundation subjects – history, geography, art, design technology, RE (except in faith schools, which tend to allocate 10%) and music and drama, if they still appear on the curriculum – will be given 5% of curriculum time each, or approximately 45-50 hours of curriculum time per year. However, it's not uncommon to see music, art and drama given one hour of curriculum time per week, reducing the total to nearer 35 hours each. Many schools are satisfied with this approach.

However, schools may decide that Year 9 pupils should be allowed to go deeper into fewer subjects – depth is given an increased priority. In Year 9, instead of providing pupils with 5% curriculum time for each of art, drama, music and design technology, we provided 10% curriculum time or approximately 90-100 hours for each subject. Pupils opted for one of the subjects, sacrificing breadth for greater depth. Similarly, pupils opted for either history or geography, studying one in greater depth for 10% of the curriculum. The third option block, again allowing 10% curriculum time, enabled pupils to opt for the other humanities subject, or a second art/technology subject, or a second MFL or computer science.

As a leader, I chose to limit the shallowing of the curriculum in Year 9, whereas others would limit the narrowing of it. It's important to note that this is a separate debate to the starting of GCSEs early, at the beginning of Year 9. The three-year key stage 3 exists purely because GCSEs and O-levels before them were teachable in two years; this is arguably no longer the case.

The curriculum challenge then passes to each subject leader: greater breadth or depth within a subject? In designing a curriculum as a middle leader and teaching it, the number of concepts, ideas, books, artists, composers and time periods to be covered – and to what depth – is a key professional determination. The more content you decide to cover, the less time available to cover each aspect; depth is sacrificed for breadth. The current educational discourse would have you believe there is a right answer. However, broader and shallower or narrower and deeper depends on too many issues to be a binary decision. It's complex.

CHAPTER 12
The Great Pause

Returning to a familiar idea, we are in a liminal space – a disorientating time between the world that has been and the world that may be. These are times that are so profoundly discontinuous that we reconsider the purpose of our lives: to what extent has my life been well lived? The worldwide pause caused by the Covid-19 pandemic is our generation's Great Pause. We are likely to re-enter the world changed.

Rohr (2020) sees a parallel between our current experiences and the initiation process. Initiation processes have existed throughout time and across many cultures. They mark the shift from childhood to adulthood. No longer do we see life from our egocentric teenage perspective: "This is my life. I can do what I want." We move into a bigger world, a more complex world that involves many others. An adult world in which we can create life and we are responsible for the lives and wellbeing of others.

This gives our lives greater meaning and purpose – the relatedness that comes from connecting, interacting and caring for others. Rohr (2020) identifies five essential messages of initiation: "Life is hard; you are not important; your life is not about you; you are not in control; you are going to die." These messages are not an easy read but they are a necessary read. They challenge the immature, competitive, self-serving selves and systems we exist in. They are a call to be *more* than we currently are.

In part, I would describe this "more" as ensuring a preferential option for the poor, keeping closest to our hearts the most vulnerable, disadvantaged and damaged within our society. Every school, leader and teacher makes a contribution to this, for better or for worse, irrespective of their school's particular demographic. It is about recognising our interdependence and connectedness as educators, alongside individual responsibilities. We are responsible for the lives well lived of all our nation's children and young people, not just those with whom we come into daily contact. For this to become a lived reality will require a substantial re-purposing of our current education system.

Leading up to the general election in 2015, I coordinated the writing of a pamphlet, on behalf of the SSAT, titled *A Vision for Education – beyond five-year policy cycles*. It was written in a narrative style, describing the changes we envisioned for the education system from the perspective of a woman who was a newly qualified teacher in 2015. The first part of the story followed her early career, in an increasingly fractured and dysfunctional education system, until that system imploded in 2020. This was a literary device to encourage the setting up of a royal commission to rethink the purpose of schooling. Key strands of thinking around school structures, the educational and social dimensions of a school, teacher agency and proportionate accountability all featured in the pamphlet. It contained 10 concrete proposals, the first being the need for a "national conversation". It is now time for that national conversation.

In 2004, the OECD produced a document that proposed six scenarios for schools, titled *The Schooling Scenarios*. I remember presenting these to governors and senior leaders at our annual development planning meeting, about 15 years ago, with the intention of promoting thinking and discussion about the school we wanted to be.

There were two "status quo" propositions. The first, the meltdown scenario, was built around the system's inability to retain and recruit sufficient teachers. We are increasingly facing the impact of this as a reality. The second, the bureaucratic scenario, imagined schools as part of a national system that had complex administrative arrangements, was largely resistant to change, had limited funding, and was subject to frequent criticism from politicians and parts of the media. You can see the prevalence of both these scenarios during the past decade and at the start of this new one.

The two "re-schooling" scenarios are particularly interesting. One looks at schools as learning-focused organisations; the other considers schools as social centres. The past 10 years have seen the first scenario flourish and the second merely survive against the cuts brought about by austerity. Schools as learning-focused organisations were based on a "strong knowledge rather than social agenda" (OECD, 2004). I think it is fair to say that has been a key direction of travel since 2010. However, other key aspects of the learning-focused scenario have not been realised: equality of opportunity as the norm; substantial investment, especially in disadvantaged communities; equal access to ICT; and favourable working conditions for teachers.

The real pressure point over the past decade has been schools' work as core social centres. The need has never been greater, but the funding and the accountability systems have conspired to limit schools' ability to act as "the most effective bulwark against fragmentation in society and the family"

(OECD, 2004). The OECD was clear that this scenario required "generous levels of financial support". There was anything but between 2010-20, with the period between 2015 and 2020 particularly severe. Schools experienced significant real-terms cuts to budgets and the continued decimation of local authorities. The reality is that this hit the poorest the hardest.

I can look back on many decisions I took with governors, directors and senior leaders, over the years, to build enhanced capacity and capability within our schools to meet the needs of many of our children and young people, particularly the most vulnerable and disadvantaged. But with regret, in the final few years of my career I had to: reduce the number of hours of speech and language therapy available to our youngest children; no longer part-fund a police community support officer; and gradually run down the children's centre, attached to one of the schools. The last was due to funding changes at local authority level determined by national funding policies. None of these was desirable. All had a negative impact upon our work as a "bulwark against fragmentation in society and the family".

The final two OECD scenarios were described as "de-schooling". These proposed another way to educate children and young people that involved either learning networks and the network society or an extension of the market model. Both were predicated on radical changes to the current model of schooling – five days a week via public funding – and the traditional role of teachers.

The first de-schooling scenario was built around small groups, increased homeschooling and individualised arrangements based on "diverse parental, cultural, religious and community interests". It required inexpensive and powerful ICT capacity. The combination of the internet of things, high connectivity, cloud storage, big data and the increased capability of artificial intelligence all make this scenario more possible now than when it was first proposed. The second de-schooling scenario, the market model, was conceived around multiple new and diverse providers enabled by very different funding mechanisms, providing direct competition to schools.

During the Great Pause, people have had time to rethink and experience different ways of living and working. Not all of it has been positive; in fact, some aspects have been awful. However, those who have got used to homeworking may want their post-Covid work/home arrangements to be very different: no more long commutes; the flexibility to fit work in around other commitments, instead of being chained to the 9-5; and more time to spend with children and loved ones. This might accelerate a shift to a more flexible way of schooling. This was already present in society pre-lockdown, but the desire for a better work/home balance for families and a more blended style of learning for pupils, particularly as they get older, may have increased.

It's important to note these OECD scenarios. Some people are now calling for a reimagining of schooling and education. Much of what is being proposed has, in fact, already been imagined and for some time. What is actually required is the re-purposing of schools. This requires personal, professional and political decision-making. Political in the sense that parliament and the elected government have substantial powers, but also political in terms of the sovereignty of the people. The government rules with the consent of the people and we collectively have a legitimate right to be involved in the important debate around the purpose of education. It is not something delegated to politicians to decide.

When talking about the creation of a "master-work", Matthew Arnold (1864) believed that there were two important factors at play: "the power of the man and the power of the moment". The moment is the determining factor. I sense that we are witnessing that moment – the pandemic has created it. The issues that need addressing were already present in the system; they are not new, but the need to re-purpose education has been exposed. Renewal is a process, not just an event. It takes time. And with limited capacity and resource within the system, the start of the process might initially involve letting go of a number of practices.

There are two interrelated elements in the process of re-purposing that it is paramount to hold in our minds. First, we need universal improvements to the system that will benefit all children and young people, including those from disadvantaged backgrounds. Second, we need a series of bespoke responses to improve outcomes for the long-term disadvantaged.

The Covid-19 pandemic has exposed many of these underlying issues to a greater number of people. It did not cause them. Changes to the curriculum, over the past decade, have significantly enhanced the potential intellectual development of pupils. However, they have also led to an overemphasis on testing substantial amounts of content. This is not only damaging learning, from a knowledge perspective, but it has also led to a narrowing of what it means to educate. Reducing curriculum content would enable teaching for mastery and consequentially lead to a reduction in the burdensome and narrow testing system. Re-purposing the curriculum would allow for greater balance and a focus on the holistic development of the child.

The social and emotional development of children, at a system level, is given insufficient importance. A culture of pupil compliance, in the absence of the necessary compassion and understanding, is causing harm. Key to the success of these alterations would be concurrent changes to our pernicious, high-stakes and narrow accountability system. The greatest beneficiaries would be those in our most disadvantaged communities, who disproportionately experience the most unhelpful and damaging impact of the current system.

CHAPTER 13
Context matters

For a number of years, I've had the privilege of speaking at the Festival of Education at Wellington College, Berkshire. Opened in the 1850s, the school was built as a national monument to the Duke of Wellington. The buildings and grounds are historic and magnificent; it's difficult not to be impressed. I'm not quite sure what it takes to be a successful teacher or leader at Wellington College. I doubt I have it. The contrast between Wellington and my work in Blackpool is stark. Blackpool is not for everyone either. Purpose is impacted by context.

Blackpool is an extreme town in terms of deprivation. By way of example, lower layer super output areas (LSOAs) consist of geographical areas that together have a population of 6,000-9,000 people. Across England and Wales there are just under 35,000 LSOAs. When these are ranked according to the level of deprivation, eight out of the 10 most deprived areas are in Blackpool. The long-term disadvantaged are hugely over-represented in the town's schools.

Here is the data for the three schools in the trust of which I was CEO:

- St Mary's (an 11-18 secondary school) has 23% of pupils from the bottom 1% of the most deprived areas in England and Wales, using data from the Index of Multiple Deprivation (IMD). 82% of pupils are from the bottom third of the most deprived areas.
- Christ the King and St Cuthbert's (both one-form-entry primary schools) have 58% and 31% of pupils from the bottom 1% of the most deprived areas, respectively. Both have more than 80% of pupils from the bottom third of the most deprived areas.

This creates not simply a large number of people living in poverty, but a depth of poverty that can be difficult to grasp. Families are not just poor. They are among the poorest of the poor.

As is the practice at many schools, my career ended with the traditional leaving speech. This is an extract from my speech:

"At the end of my 20 years of stewardship, we are making up more food hampers for our families than ever before, organising vouchers for heating, lighting and cooking. For the first time ever, we are opening up our schools over Christmas and the New Year to the families in our communities who we are called to serve. It's possibly not quite what I imagined leading a school would be like all those years ago.

Yet clearing out the office, on a set of overhead projector transparencies I found the presentation I did when being interviewed for the headteacher post. One transparency talked of a distinctive school and my notes read 'collaboration with other schools' and 'a place for the poor/a contribution beyond league tables'. Maybe I did have a sense of what I was being called to do, but simply hadn't yet experienced the daily lived reality of Blackpool. It's an experience that brings knowledge beyond theory. Praxis – theory plus action – brings that much deeper understanding all of you have."

The previous month had been a whirlwind focused on *The Sunday Times* Christmas Appeal, operated in association with the Education Endowment Foundation. The appeal raised more than £1 million for schools working in the most socioeconomically deprived areas of England. Alongside Sarah Smith (executive headteacher of Christ the King and St Cuthbert's Catholic Academies, Blackpool) and Roger Farley (headteacher at Westminster Primary Academy, Blackpool), we took receipt of an initial £30,000 to help provide for local families at Christmas.

The Sunday Times' reporting had exposed to a nationwide audience the daily reality of many of our families. In a freezing December, some families had no money to switch the heating on. Food cupboards and fridges were empty. Some families had no ovens or beds or sufficient appropriate clothing. What is required to build the necessary social capital may vary from community to community. What was required in Blackpool was to meet basic needs first.

With an agreed shopping list, and having transferred £6,000 to AldiUK, we took six minibuses and 20 staff to the local store to collect the contents of hundreds of food parcels. These parcels were packed up by staff and children in the various schools before being given to families. They were supplemented by a supply of fresh meat – mince, sausages, bacon – that didn't require an oven in order to be cooked.

In addition, £9,000 of fuel vouchers were distributed to ensure sufficient gas and electricity to heat homes and cook food over the Christmas period. The schools opened up for various days over the festive period; staff, plus the odd volunteer from the local community or afar, ensured activities were provided, as well as a hot meal at midday and emotional support where needed.

These challenges are exacerbated by many things. At school level, funding is a huge issue. If you compare Blackpool to other similar areas in London, you begin to get a sense of the inequality. For St Mary's, the difference in budget is around £2.8 million per annum. Over the 14 years of my headship at the school, that comes to a budget difference of just under £40 million. That is substantial and makes a significant difference to the capacity available to meet the additional needs of pupils.

Resources are needed but also an emphasis, within the education provided, that addresses the sense of helplessness and lack of personal empowerment felt by many. There is also a sense of hopelessness: why bother nothing will change? And a sense of homelessness: there is little feeling of belonging when you have been pushed out to the edge of society. You no longer feel like a citizen or have a stake in a society that has rejected you. Personal empowerment and the need to generate a sense of citizenship take on a great importance. Education needs to help you find a reason for living as well as a way of earning a living.

Although autonomy may remove external rules or restrictions that unnecessarily limit our freedoms as individuals or organisations, too often the limits we experience come from within. They are self-imposed. Agency is about removing these internal barriers that are often rooted in fear. This then enables a person to overcome the external barriers, or simply not recognise them as blocks to taking greater control of their own life. This lack of agency, experienced by many of our children and young people, needs to be addressed. It is one of the reasons that many of us came into education.

David Lammy MP has told the powerful story of his friend Khadija Saye. On 14 June 2017, she was 24 years old, a photographer with a growing reputation and a resident of the 20th floor of Grenfell Tower, West London. On that fateful night, Saye, like many other residents, was told to stay in her flat. She stayed as the fire took hold and sadly took her life. Lammy's view was that if people are or feel systematically disempowered by the system, this impacts significantly on their personal agency. If someone in a suit or uniform tells you to do something, you tend to do it. This had a terrible impact at Grenfell Tower.

The appalling loss of life at Grenfell wasn't about a lack of knowledge. The heart-wrenching phone calls from people staying put in the tower, to their families, friends and loved ones, suggest they knew what was happening. Instinctively, they would have known what to do, but they were told to go against those instincts by people in positions of authority. This lack of personal empowerment contributed to the tragic loss of life.

A lack of agency will be particularly prevalent in various disadvantaged communities or those that, over time, have experienced institutionalised or systematic discrimination. Life control is the belief that by your actions you can direct how you live your life. In Blackpool, it is significantly lower owing to the helplessness that deep poverty can cause. Not everyone is or feels empowered. This is a challenge to any system that fails to give appropriate priority, in schools, to the empowerment of each person.

Too many people still cling to accountability as the answer to school improvement. The metrics used within the system are too narrow and too imperfect. They are not fit for purpose. What is really needed is a focus on enhanced life outcomes for everyone, in every community – lives well lived. It is issue of deep social justice, not just school improvement. This is unlikely to be resolved by simplistic, counterproductive school grading and performance tables.

Schools are part of the fabric of a local community, in all areas, particularly those that suffer from deep socioeconomic disadvantage. There is a need for sufficient high-quality social, health, policing and housing provision, as well as connectedness. There is a need for greater equity. Our poor are too poor. They suffer from so many inequalities, the greatest of which is a lack of money. While society decides whether it wants to change, schools remain on the frontline.

> *"But there are limits to what teachers can do in an increasingly unequal environment outside the school gates. The drive to close attainment gaps is doomed to failure. We need a rethink – agreeing what basics all children need and nurturing wider child outcomes that matter in life. And we must, if nothing else, develop teachers as expert practitioners, combining best bets with local knowledge."*   Major (2019)

The lack of "local knowledge" in our systems and processes is severely limiting attempts to improve the lives and life chances of those in our most disadvantaged communities. It is created by the exclusion of those who lead and have led schools in the most disadvantaged communities from contributing to the debate, at a system level.

Dan Heath (2020) states: "Every system is perfectly designed to get the results it gets." Our accountability system is designed to limit the opportunities for those schools and school leaders serving the greatest number of vulnerable and disadvantaged children and young people. The opportunities afforded to Teaching Schools and National Leaders of Education are limited to those schools Ofsted considers to be outstanding. Inspection grades are highly correlated with the affluence of a school's intake.

CHAPTER 14
How to help the long-term disadvantaged?

My work over the decades – successes and failures – has been aligned with the long-term disadvantaged, particularly those who identify as white British. The lack of progress of this group of pupils is depressingly similar across the country, yet rarely is it a focus at a national level. The impact of this underperformance plays into an accountability system in which the schools with the largest percentage of this sub-group are over-represented among the schools graded as inadequate and under-represented (if represented at all) among those graded as outstanding. As a consequence, teachers from these schools are more likely to leave the school and the profession, leaving the schools facing the greatest challenge even less well placed to meet it.

Plaister and Thomson (2019) of FFT Education Datalab analysed how white British long-term disadvantaged pupils had performed in London compared with the same cohort in other regions – the London effect disappears.

Blackpool epitomises this great unanswered challenge in our education system: how can we help the long term disadvantaged to succeed? No one has yet managed to answer this question.

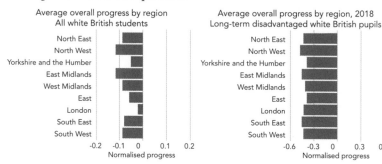

(Source: FFT Education Datalab)

Much of the difference in performance between various regions in England can simply be explained by the varying numbers of long-term disadvantaged pupils. The political and media headlines extolling the virtues of education in the South of England and decrying education in the North are simply diversionary hot air.

Long-term disadvantage is defined as being eligible for free school meals for 80% or more of your time in school. The needs of this group of children and young people aren't purely intellectual – schools need to help counteract the exponential impact of poverty. Expecting schools to lead on this is practical and sensible. Parents are legally required to educate their children and this predominantly happens within schools. We have eyes on and interaction with the overwhelming majority of children, young people and their families. So it is important to create schools in which children and young people from disadvantaged backgrounds feel empowered and their needs and aspirations are considered relevant.

Many of the challenges have been brutally exposed during the Covid-19 lockdown. Those of us used to working in disadvantaged communities are amazed that the following are suddenly considered newsworthy, because we've known about them for years: the digital divide; disadvantaged pupils not spending as long on their studies; food poverty; the impact of domestic violence; a lack of outside or recreational space; and poor mental health. These challenges have appeared in surveys and research ad nauseam.

Added to this is the increased number of children and young people who are suffering bereavements. This will affect all communities and all schools. As ever, these issues hit the poorest communities, which have a higher level of underlying health issues, the hardest. Salford, a very disadvantaged area in Manchester, was reporting triple the number of deaths from Covid-19 than Trafford, a more advantaged area right next to it. Disadvantaged communities with a high number of people from BAME backgrounds appear to be even more affected.

If we are ever to address these issues successfully, schools need to be "generously funded" (OECD, 2004) to act as core social centres. Like many of the Treasury's efforts to support the economy during the pandemic, it would be an investment now to save money in the long term. However, it's not a job schools can do on their own. I helped to write Headteachers' Roundtable's *The Alternative Green Paper* (2016), which made a series of recommendations that placed schools within a wider infrastructure of coordinated support. I summarise those proposals here:

The government, working in partnership with local authorities, should establish a set of cross-departmental policies to support children and their families, with associated funding, over a 10-year period, in the first instance. The explicit aim would be to increase the number of pupils from disadvantaged backgrounds accessing level 3 qualifications at 16 years of age. The policies should command cross-party support, so regardless of the political party in power, all public services will have a clear long-term focus on reducing social inequality by improving educational attainment outcomes.

This cross-departmental work should link better housing, greater support to address mental health issues and the root causes (for example, addiction or domestic abuse), and early and ongoing parenting skills. The policy focus should be on ensuring connected, focused working in schools of workers from pupil welfare, social services, health and the police.

Key is a national inter-agency parent support strategy supporting all parents to create an optimal home-learning environment for under-fives. While targeting this initially at families in socioeconomically deprived communities, our aspiration is to establish universal entitlements to services that help all parents to maximise their children's health, wellbeing and learning in the period before they arrive at school. Parents who need support to develop their child's language development, self-esteem, school readiness and broader aspirations should have access to education-orientated services in their communities.

Our view was that policies should be informed by research, regularly and rigorously monitored, and changed in response to the findings of the monitoring, rather than in response to a change of government or political leadership. Addressing the issues experienced by the long-term disadvantaged will require some radical thinking – "a stream of fresh and free thought upon our stock notions and habits" (Arnold, 1869). A wide range of entangled issues need to be considered, many of which will apply to other ethnic groups besides the white British.

As discussed in chapter 11, Allen (2019) and White (2019) use the term "wicked problem" (borrowed from policy research) to describe the problem of school improvement. According to Allen and White, wicked problems and their solutions have a number of discernible characteristics, which I would summarise as:

- A wicked problem is "intractable" and "impossible to fully solve". Hence, it is better to focus on constituent issues where causal links and improvements can be made (i.e. improving phonics rather than solving illiteracy).

- The essence of the wicked problem appears differently to different stakeholders. The different presentations of the problem lead to the proposal of "alternative plausible solutions". The accompanying internally coherent perfect solution is actually a partial, imperfect, potential solution.
- The relative vagueness of the perfect solution proposed, in empirical terms, and disparate application means it is difficult or impossible for it to be robustly evaluated. Rhetoric trumps evidence for a period of time.
- However, over time the lack of impact or previously unforeseen distortions caused by the perfect solution lead to the problem being regularly redefined and alternative solutions proposed.

Addressing the challenge of improving educational outcomes and the life chances of the long-term disadvantaged would fit this description. Simple, practical, implementable policy proposals are key to supporting politicians to move forward on these complex issues. Vague exhortations are of little value.

As a headteacher, I decided to put £1 per day on the dinner card of every pupil who was entitled to a free school meal. At the end of each day, if the £1 wasn't spent, it dropped off the pupil's total. It was a very simple decision to ensure that every pupil could have both breakfast and lunch. I didn't overcomplicate it by limiting it to the healthier items available. It was just access to food for those who were most likely to be hungry.

The Manchester United footballer Marcus Rashford has spoken openly about being hungry as a child and used his status to highlight the issue of food poverty. In partnership with FareShare, a food distribution charity, he helped to raise more than £20 million during the Covid-19 lockdown, allowing the charity to distribute the equivalent of more than three million meals each week. Rashford's heartfelt campaign, rooted in experience, brought about a government U-turn on funding meals for disadvantaged children during the 2020 summer holidays. Now, the families of circa 1.25 million children, entitled to free school meals, will receive food vouchers to cover the six-week summer break.

> *"This is not about politics; this is about humanity. Looking at ourselves in the mirror and feeling like we did everything we could to protect those who can't, for whatever reason or circumstance, protect themselves. Political affiliations aside, can we not all agree that no child should be going to bed hungry?"*
> Marcus Rashford's open letter to MPs (15 June 2020)

This could become a simple-to-implement policy at a national level: pay an additional amount direct to disadvantaged families, to give each child or young person a main meal every day during school holidays. The state has long accepted the responsibility for providing a free lunch to children and young people from disadvantaged homes during term time. This would merely be an extension to full-year provision. The cost per eligible pupil would be £200 per annum (£15 per week over 13 weeks of school holidays, plus £5 bonus at Christmas, likely to be used for electricity or gas). The money could be paid directly to families as part of the benefits system, or given as a series of vouchers covering periods of school closure. Far more families are likely to be supported by the benefits system during the early years of this decade. The benefits of good nutrition will positively impact many areas of life.

Given the work done by those in the care and delivery sectors during the pandemic, and the increased esteem in which their work is held in, a significant increase in the national living wage or the removal of zero-hours contracts could be other policy responses. These are implementable proposals that could decrease levels of poverty and support the work of schools in improving educational outcomes.

Many of the "plausible solutions" (Allen, 2019) to long-term poverty are often part of a narrative about social mobility. In our most deprived communities, social mobility often involves climbing up the socioeconomic ladder by moving out of the area. Leaving Blackpool may help the individual to have a more successful life, but it weakens the overall community. Place-based change needs to be built on the wider concept of social justice. It is about lifting the whole community out of poverty. As the term suggests, this is about justice – what is right and good – not charity. Communities need to have a voice in the process. To create fairer schools, you need a more equitable society; to create a fairer society, you need more equitable schools. Education both leads and reflects the society in which it is sited.

Solutions to closing the disadvantage gap will be found both inside and outside education. This demonstrates the close interdependence between education and health, nutrition, housing, social services, policing, community safety and welfare, and the economic health of each family. Closing the many gaps exposed, emphasised and widened by the Covid-19 pandemic are at the root of greater educational equity.

When it comes to policies more directly applicable to the education system, Dylan Wiliam has already done some of the thinking for us. In his book *Creating the Schools Our Children Need* (2018), he calls into question much of the current orthodoxy, such as school choice, policy tourism and performance-related pay. His conclusions are that the curriculum and improving the teachers we have are the two universal approaches to helping improve education for all.

CHAPTER 15
Re-purposing the curriculum

In uncompromising statements reported by *Tes* (Lough, 2020), Dylan Wiliam describes the teaching of a content-heavy curriculum as "immoral" because "it leaves the majority of pupils behind". He is concerned that curriculum developers tend to overfill the curriculum to ensure no child has "spare time on their hands", leading to a curriculum suited to the fast-learning pupils, with far too much content for most pupils to assimilate.

One of the curriculum principles proposed by Wiliam (2013) is that of focus. He defines this as the extent to which the curriculum is manageable. This requires the teaching of the most important knowledge – the big ideas or key concepts within a subject. Over the past decade, the increased importance of knowledge within the curriculum has arguably also led to the idea of "the more, the better".

We are reaching the point where we are in danger of fetishising content – a tunnel view where the only way is forward and we don't have a stop or a pause button (Heath, 2020). The risk of some of the more extreme views about content in the curriculum is that you lose sight of the fundamentals. Knowledge can be beautiful in its own right and knowledge may be useful in our lives. Either way, it has to be *learned*, not just encountered at an increasingly frenetic pace.

There is only so much time. As such, the most difficult curriculum decision is always what to leave out. Too much content can be counterproductive to learning. The main obsession for the teacher is curriculum coverage – a fast pace and moving on to what is next are key. Curriculum content also has to be considered alongside what is consequentially missed out. What is being missed may be of greater importance to telos.

In a fascinating blog, Solomon Kingsnorth (2019) compares the 2015 PISA outcomes for mathematics among students in Estonia, a high-performing country that ranks just below the Pacific Rim powerhouses, with the more moderate outcomes for English students. He starts by looking into what he sees as the alarming number of incorrect answers in GCSE mathematics papers:

> " ... *after 12 years of schooling, regular exam practice and weeks of cramming – at the very point when children should know the most, seventy-five percent of students got around 60–100% of their maths questions wrong.*" Kingsnorth (2019)

He does not blame schools or teachers. Rather, his hypothesis is that "the national curriculum, from Year 1 to Year 11, is too big for large-scale mastery". Further, he suggests that the size of the current national curriculum "is discriminatory towards those with poorer fluid intelligence and working memory, and will forever get in the way of mass fluency until it is reduced". He sees this as the key problem to be addressed.

Fluid intelligence is the capacity to reason and solve problems, as opposed to crystalline intelligence, which is more dependent on what we already know. Fluid intelligence naturally varies across the population. Those with high fluid intelligence process new information much more rapidly than those with lower fluid intelligence. Both are capable of learning the same information, but those with lower fluid memory need longer. The packed national curriculum in England is more accessible to those with high fluid intelligence. For others, the need to cover so much information in such a short amount of time means they fail to master the concepts taught before the teacher moves on. The curriculum has reached what Kingsnorth refers to as the Goldilocks Plateau – "that point beyond which not everyone can master all of the content".

The issue of mastering the content is therefore one of sufficient time per objective/threshold concept. In some of the countries at the top of the PISA rankings, this sufficient time is provided by private tutoring and evening classes. But Estonia's relative success is not based on increased time, rather on "boil[ing] the curriculum down to key threshold concepts, and spend[ing] more time mastering them" (Kingsnorth, 2019). Estonia's equivalent of our GCSE has more than 80% less content, giving five times the time to master each objective. There is even more time per objective in their equivalent of our key stage 2. This is a focused curriculum in action. The result is mastery of key threshold concepts for the large majority of children.

Kingsnorth suggests looking at the curriculum through the lens of three key spectrums: the level of difficulty or challenge; the number of objectives or amount of content; and the amount of time available to teach each objective. The Goldilocks principle requires the curriculum to be just right. Hitting the mastery sweet spot requires a series of decisions to be made to ensure that, within the time available, the curriculum has the right amount of challenge and content – neither too much nor too little.

The belief that all pupils should reach the same standard despite very, very different starting points needs a curriculum response. Primary and secondary schools in the most disadvantaged communities often have a larger number of pupils who need greater support with literacy and numeracy. If the content is not reduced, how do you find the time to focus on these basics? That time could be found by limiting the curriculum time available to foundation subjects or reducing the content of the English and mathematics curricula, providing more scope to develop and embed the key concepts and ideas. There's no easy choice. Too often, we opt to pretend everything is fine and plough on regardless. That just kicks the problem down the line.

In her book *Cleverlands* (2016), Lucy Crehan identifies a series of principles for high-performing, equitable education systems, including that they "design curricula concepts for mastery (and context for motivation)". The curricula she explored were:

- **Minimal**: "focusing on fewer topics, but in greater depth".
- **High level**: "clear on what concepts and skills are required, without prescribing context or pedagogy".
- **Ordered**: "organising concepts in a logical order, based on research into how children learn".

The curriculum has layers. It evolves out of the school's purpose of education. It is organised through a set of governing principles, held in tension, that give structure and priorities to the curriculum at a whole-school level and then through policy to its realisation within the classroom. It is in the classroom that you find the critical interface where the teacher and pupils interact. It is in this relationship that the curriculum is given life. The curriculum is within our area of influence. It is something over which we can exert some professional control.

The potential exists to create one of those very rare win-win situations. Reducing the content of the current curriculum in England would not only enhance cultural transmission and the learning of knowledge, but also provide the space required for other aspects of education that are, at best, on the margins of school life. This would require us to grasp the paradox that children learn more by covering less. The "less" needs to be carefully selected, connected and sequenced, and linked to a purpose. Cultural and disciplinary knowledge need to be sufficient to ensure coherence and sufficiently limited to be learned by the majority.

There is the possibility, as schools open to more pupils post-Covid-19, to rethink our approach to the content-heavy curriculum. It will be an acute issue for pupils starting Years 11 and 13 in September 2020, but the solution is applicable to all pupils and year groups.

Re-purposing the curriculum will require us to consider the dynamic interactivity of content, pedagogy and the learner, in the teaching process. Each may be considered as a distinct separate entity, but to make sense of the whole we need to consider them together. These entangled aspects are further entwined with overall purpose and human relationships.

CHAPTER 16
Re-purposing social
and emotional development

The prevailing narrative, linked to a cultural transmission philosophy, is that pupils must work hard. This is not unreasonable. In fact, I'd suggest it is necessary. Unfortunately, this too often becomes confused with a wider inappropriate narrative about the feckless poor and the need to pull ourselves up by our bootstraps.

This narrative fails to recognise that many disadvantaged families are hard-working and responsible. They have far fewer means (bootstraps) than those of us who are affluent, privileged and connected. Dr Lee Elliot Major, professor of social mobility at Exeter University, speaking at the SSAT National Conference 2019, described how social mobility doesn't happen at the extremes of the socioeconomic continuum. The super-rich and super-poor are static at the top and bottom, respectively. Social mobility happens across the middle of the spectrum. Social justice requires us to enable and empower the most disadvantaged.

There is an increasing tendency, in some schools, to prioritise organisational needs and only deal with individual social and emotional needs at the point of crisis – or simply move challenging pupils on. This is a purpose issue, deeply rooted in a view of both society and humanity. Our education system needs to reflect and live out our beliefs about what it is to be human and how we live as an individual within a community – the "I" and the "we". There is a need to rebalance, so we don't lose the individual in the structures and processes. We need to prevent the creation of a depersonalised system, which can happen in different ways, but a school's behaviour policy and practice is an obvious place for it to start.

Behaviour has always been an emotive subject in schools. Teachers face the daily reality, for better or worse, of classroom behaviour. Parents experience it through their children who are perpetrators or victims, sometimes both. It can be too easy for those in senior leadership positions, if divorced from the daily maelstrom of the classroom, to look back with rose-tinted glasses or forget the level of challenge that poor behaviour can bring. Some children and young people make bad choices and continue to do so until they are permanently excluded. Unlike many others who comment on the process of exclusion, I have been in the position where the final decision rested with me. It was never an easy decision. I needed to be able to look myself in the mirror and know that I made the right and just decision, for the community and the individual.

My preferred behaviour system is one that is effective (gets pupils to behave very well), inclusive (doesn't allow schools to move the most vulnerable and disadvantaged pupils elsewhere) and designed and implemented out of love for an individual and others in the community. This provides the essential tension required in the system.

Without this essential tension, some schools begin to move towards unethical behaviours. The strong fail in their duty to look after those who are most needy in our society. One of the latest unethical behaviours is the movement of increasing numbers of pupils into elective home education. This is a safeguarding disaster waiting to happen. Not for the children whose parents have made a lifestyle and educational choice – they have the capacity to deliver effectively. Rather, my concern is for the poor and the marginalised, who some schools feel they need to push out to protect headline performance table measures.

Another concerning approach to behaviour management is termed "flattening the grass". It involves senior leaders going into a newly sponsored school with the expressed aim of forcing out pupils who are anything less than compliant.

Previously, less overt means led to similar outcomes: some schools sought only retain those pupils who were compliant and made good progress, while pressurising others to move on. There's little reward for those schools that take the pupils other schools are desperate to lose. They are the educators of last resort.

There are schools where poor behaviour has become endemic and the situation rightly needs tackling. But exclusion can be inappropriately used by some schools, which continue to have high levels of exclusion long after the "turnaround phase". The intention appears to be cohort change – the manipulation of the performance tables and the inspectorate. The unnecessarily high exclusion rates become a proxy for school improvement, to the long-term detriment of the school and most certainly the people in the locality. A faux, unscalable school improvement process has been spawned. Some of these schools may have been doing this for so long that it has become habitual; they may have managed to convince themselves that it is appropriate and right.

A lack of empowerment and capacity means the families of these pushed-out pupils have limited ability to challenge the practices. Statistically, such pupils are far more likely to be male and from disadvantaged backgrounds. The idea that the permanent exclusion process provides a secure route for parents to argue their case is the product of a middle-class mind. For some of our most deprived and disadvantaged families, it provides nothing of the sort. They lack the capacity, confidence or capability to use the system.

Passing on the responsibility for our most vulnerable, disadvantaged and challenging children and young people – as a school, system or society – will not end well. As equity dips, people diverge and a more fractured and confrontational society is formed. Ultimately, we won't be judged on our latest Progress 8 or combined RWM score, but on how we treat those in greatest need.

> *"Let all bear in mind that a society is judged not so much by the standards attained by its more affluent and privileged members as by the quality of life which it is able to assure for its weakest members."* Javier Pérez de Cuéllar

Blackpool's continuum of provision

It might have been more accurate to use the subheading "Blackpool's lack of continuum of provision". The impact of austerity and massively reduced capacity at local authority level, combined with real-terms cuts to school funding, extreme levels of poverty and needy and disadvantaged families moving into Blackpool, have led to decimated provision and overstretched, limited capacity. Additionally, a significant amount of school capacity, disproportionately high compared with other areas, is required for ongoing safeguarding.

In Blackpool's schools, provision for pupils with high or multiple needs is very limited. This leads to a tendency to remove the "problem child", rather than address the problems experienced by the child. A binary option exists for pupils: mainstream or alternative provision.

Historically, the number of pupils in alternative provision is statistically higher in Blackpool than other local authorities. Between September 2014 and May 2019, 228 pupils were permanently excluded from Blackpool secondary schools. This is approximately twice the rate of permanent exclusions compared with statistical neighbours and four times the rate of permanent exclusions nationally. The number of exclusions between Blackpool secondary schools varied massively.

In addition, 203 pupils were considered by the in-year fair access panel (which deals with the most difficult-to-place children and young people) between September 2016 and April 2019. More than 75% were from outside Blackpool. Of the total number, 72 were placed in alternative provision. These numbers led to the formation of a project, jointly funded by the local authority and opportunity area board, to address the underlying concerns.

The project followed an extended period of discussion between the local authority and various multi-academy trust CEOs and headteachers about the delegation of funding and responsibility for alternative provision. The situation had hit an impasse, partly due to the very high number of permanent exclusions by some schools. Their financial liabilities would not have been covered by the increased funding. With another year of excessively high permanent exclusions and elective home education numbers going in the wrong direction, I offered to lead discussions about creating a continuum of provision to support high-needs pupils. The first meeting was for the CEOs of the secondary academies. It was an invitation to a "blood on the walls" meeting.

The "blood on the walls" meeting was actually very well-mannered and pretty calm. The issues of behaviour and equitable distribution of the most challenging pupils between schools are hugely emotive ones. It was important that we allowed all the angst to be put on the table, allowed people to have their say and allowed unacceptable behaviour to be called out. There was a lot less blood than I expected – a few points and counter-points – and a very rapid move to focus on how we put in place enhanced provision.

For whatever reason, a number of Blackpool secondary schools had substantially higher numbers of fixed-term and permanent exclusions than all or similar schools. Exclusions were not related to levels of deprivation – schools with very similar numbers of pupils from disadvantaged backgrounds had dramatically different exclusion rates. The baseline data collected from the 2018/19 academic year showed: permanent exclusions – 55; elective home education – 96; and moves to other Blackpool schools – 105. A target was agreed to reduce permanent exclusions to no more than 24 in the 2019/20 academic year and we wanted to avoid pupils being moved on through other means. The rational part of the plan was always going to be easier to pull together if people accepted the direction of travel. I had already had a conversation with Dave Whitaker, director of learning at Wellspring Academy Trust in South Yorkshire (who shares his view from alternative education in chapter 10). He had a wealth and depth of experience in alternative provision and would bring the independent know-how and know-what to the project. The collective leadership challenge we faced was how to lead schools where the actual purpose of education differed depending on the pupil, rather than being an overarching organisational purpose.

The data for the monitoring period from September 2019 to the end of May 2020 was: permanent exclusions – 13 (33); elective home education – 45 (80); and moves between Blackpool schools – 51 (94). The numbers in brackets refer to totals for the same period in the previous academic year. Although there had been some intensive work around putting additional provision in place to support pupils, the significant improvement had been achieved through a "hearts and minds" approach. As so often, when we believe something and commit to it, change happens.

Our colleagues in alternative provision work with the most disadvantaged, vulnerable and traumatised. The best of alternative provision is a joy to behold. The schools work with children and young people battered by life, rejected and in some cases further damaged by their mainstream experiences. They slowly piece them back together, supporting them as they move on in life. These children and young people need the unconditional positive regard and clear boundaries found in high-quality alternative provision. It was Dave's knowledge of trauma-informed practice, and that of his team, that was crucial to moving the project from an agreed purpose to actual practice.

The increased social and emotional aspects of education required for many pupils with high or multiple needs demand mainstream schools to show flexibility. They must run with multiple purposes under one roof. This is no easy task. It requires matching purpose for these pupils with the best of what is traditionally seen in alternative provision. That purpose is far more likely to be underpinned by an emphasis on personal empowerment and preparation for citizenship. Cultural transmission, an important aspect of mainstream education, consequently has a lower priority.

Universal provision

Although there is a need for bespoke provision for a minority of pupils, a focus on social, emotional and mental health is a universal need. Across the secondary academies and pupil referral unit in Blackpool, key stage 3 pupils have taken the GL Assessment Pupil Attitudes to Self and School (PASS) questionnaire for a number of years. This seeks to identify attitudinal or emotional issues in children before they impact on performance at school.

Its use speaks volumes about the importance attached to the emotional wellbeing of young people by these schools. Substantially lower scores across a range of measures have led to various programmes being put in place for vulnerable learners, beyond those at more immediate risk of permanent exclusion. This is about getting behind the visible symptoms of failure at school, in an attempt to address the underlying causes. It is also about ensuring the mental health and wellbeing of all children, including those who are academically successful but emotionally less secure.

When we analyse data from across Blackpool, pupils' feelings about school (whether they feel secure, confident and included) are relatively negative and attitudes to attendance (a good predictor of actual future attendance) worsen significantly over time. Learner self-regard (equivalent to self-worth) and their responses to the curriculum also decline worryingly. These last two aspects of PASS are linked to levels of motivation and determination. The purpose and content of education, in these long-term disadvantaged communities, need to include a greater focus on the attitudinal, emotional and social aspects of learning.

After launching *A Vision for Education – beyond five-year policy cycles* (SSAT, 2015), I was approached by a guy called Graham. He had enjoyed my short presentation and offered a free day-long workshop to one of the schools in our trust. It was nearly 12 months before I took him up on the offer. On the day of the workshop, I arrived in the hall to see that Graham had enlisted one of our more outspoken Year 10s as a DJ and was encouraging the year group to "get on your feet and make some noise". In contrast, I'd describe the hundreds of assemblies I had led over the years as quiet, reflective and prayerful occasions. This was out of my comfort zone. I did what any self-respecting CEO in my position would do and delegated oversight of the rest of the workshop to the school's headteacher, Simon Eccles, and his leadership team.

About an hour and a half later, I was called back to the hall. It was emotional carnage. Most of the Year 10 form tutors and pupils were in tears. What I had missed was a carefully planned session that had required our young people to talk about how they felt about school and their lives and how other people's behaviours had affected them. It was powerful beyond words. I later met Carlo, Graham's partner in crime. As we warmed to them as people but also to the power of their work, our relationship with HumanUtopia was born.

Their message was: qualifications are important – they get you the interview – but it is your character that gets you the job. Two important philosophies of education were seen as mutually supportive rather than oppositional. HumanUtopia ran a series of workshop days in various year groups, across our primary and secondary academies, most of which were led by a large group of Year 10 "Heroes". Importantly, to us, all our disadvantaged pupils either volunteered or were encouraged to become a Hero. All bar one did.

These Heroes had additional leadership training and built a whole range of skills and experiences that cannot be developed purely in the classroom. This created a tension. Staff could see the benefit, but were worried that missing a number of lessons would interrupt the pupils' learning of content, which would be potentially important to examination success. Time is finite; these tensions are real. But our belief was that a greater sense of personal empowerment would support and motivate pupils with their academic work. Many suffered from a lack of resilience when work became challenging. But there was also a purpose issue: the Year 10 Heroes were providing a service to others as well as sensing empowerment. That is a part of why we exist as schools.

It takes time, skill and a balanced purpose of education to build a bridge from what has been, for a young person, to what could be. Autonomy needs to sit alongside a growing sense of agency. The former relates to the removal of unnecessary external barriers; to a young person's sense of self-determination. The latter requires overcoming internal barriers often associated with a lack of worthiness or fear. This is the "I" of education. Children and young people need to feel and understand that they are influential determinants in their education and future direction in life.

In contrast to some of the more worrying aspects of the PASS data above, pupils' attitudes to teachers in Blackpool's schools remain high over time. Young people's perceptions of the relationships they have with the adults in school are positive. There is a "relatedness" on which to build the "we" of education. Through so many charitable activities, held over the decades, the generosity of families – many of which were the poorest in society – has shone through. Building communities and building up communities is part of the process of learning. For children and young people, it happens at a practical level; they need to feel and see social justice in action. It is a key aspect of the education we offer.

CHAPTER 17
The decade ahead

As a teacher, I always wanted the pupils I taught to do well in their examinations. It was partly my competitive nature. Also, I saw qualifications as passports to the next stage of education or training, and to a better life over time. Then there was my enthusiasm for being a form tutor and for supporting the development of the whole child. My purpose of education was holistic in nature. It was an attempt at orthopraxy (getting it right in practice) largely guided by intuition.

A similar approach flowed through my actions as a headteacher. But the absence of a theoretical underpinning meant I couldn't effectively critique my approach or my leadership. Over the years, I clarified my thinking. Doing well in your examinations is a good thing – to suggest otherwise just seems daft – but it was insufficient as an overall outcome or purpose of schooling. What I was really seeking was deep social justice and a more equitable society. A society in which it is not only possible for each person to have a life well lived, but in which this is a reality for all. Education has a part to play, but the challenge is too great to be met by schools alone.

A renewed education system

Empowering the education system to elevate and look after the most vulnerable, as its primary responsibility, doesn't come from grading the affluence of a school's intake. High-stakes accountability has run its course and is now doing more harm than good. Instead of looking to accountability to drive school improvement, we need a more holistic view of how we can improve schools and to what end. Only then can we determine the part accountability can play in improving education. What can Ofsted and performance tables do better, more reliably and to greater effect than other school improvement processes? The answer is likely to be "very little".

This fundamentally changes the power dynamic and drivers within the system. Moving schools from an unhealthy obsession with performance tables and Ofsted grades to one concerned with the poorest and most vulnerable is a necessary start. The system needs to be re-purposed and realigned. In too many parts of the system, the wrong drivers are in place. Success, job security, and enhanced pay and conditions for staff are all more likely in more advantaged areas. The system needs to be tipped on its head.

We need to recognise the very different contexts that schools find themselves in. Alongside sufficient funding for all schools, substantially enhanced funding is necessary for schools that operate in the most disadvantaged areas. If they are to be bulwarks against the worst outcomes of poverty, they need access to more high-quality services that are joined up across a locality. We need services that support families before children arrive at school and while they are at school. If we want to be more at ease with ourselves as a society – respecting of diversity in all its forms – we need to eradicate long-term poverty. This is a political decision.

A new social covenant

The concept of the social contract has long been established. As individuals, we consent to surrendering some of our freedoms to the state in exchange for the protection of other rights and the maintenance of the social order. This is both necessary and problematic. Maintaining the social order may suit the powerful much more than it suits the disenfranchised and poorest.

Contracts are often about a bottom line, a minimum expectation that needs to be met. This is an agreement that can be enforced in the courts with redress, if appropriate. It is necessary, but not enough. A different and potentially more powerful concept to guide our thinking is that of covenant. This replaces the authority within the social contract with a different driver. The relationship is at the heart of covenantal thinking. It's easy to understand this in terms of family. Like many other parents, what Cath and I have done for our family was not part of an agreement, formal or informal. It was borne out of a relationship founded in love – a relationship which understands that "we" come before "I". Cath and I "sacrificed" certain things at an individual level for the good of the whole family and gained so much more in return. Covenants are relationships formed through love and sacrifice, and maintained through reciprocity and forgiveness.

When the new Christ the King primary school and parish church were built on the site of St Mary's Catholic Academy, I coordinated a memorandum of understanding for how we would work together. In it, I described the covenantal relationship as one "conceived on the basis of our acting as one body". The covenant would only work if we had a relationship "sustained by loyalty, faithfulness, mutuality and trust".

This is a very different relationship to the ones that currently dominate our education system, both in terms of vertical and horizontal interactions. The vertical relationships include politicians, civil servants, local authority officers and schools, but also the hierarchical structures we have within schools and academy trusts. The horizontal relationships are those that exist between schools, the people who work in them and the communities they are called to serve. The power of moving from contract to covenant allows the system to become truly and profoundly collaborative. In fact, it leads the system towards a collaborative imperative. There is no definition of success built on "I". We are in a relationship. We succeed collectively or not at all.

A renewed sense of purpose

The real substance of education flows from and to the person and the people. We are created as unique individuals. We are brought fully alive in a community and must contribute to the common good. This is the "I" and "we" of life. We need an education that seeks wisdom – the ability to make good decisions. This leads to a life in which individuals may flourish, but also a life in which each person seeks to help others flourish. Or, phrased another way, we need an education that enables all to have a life well lived.

Education has to be about character and career. It is not an either/or. Reverend Stephen Chalke (2016) contends that it is "not about what you do with your life (as important as that question is). It is about something much deeper: who do you become while you are doing it?" It's the eulogy moment. What do you want people to stand up and say at your funeral? What does the hard, cold truth of your life's storyline look like? Are you happy with it or do things need to change?

At the root of our purpose of education must be the question of what it means to become more human, to become fully alive. As we debate different aspects of education, this policy and that, we are often debating our deep-rooted beliefs, values and sense of purpose.

After the Great Pause, a renewed sense of purpose is required. If we look again at cultural transmission, it is clear that the gains of the past decade, supported by the evidence around what works or at least the best bets, need to be retained. But the amount of content must be reduced, for the sake of the majority learning the necessary factual, conceptual and procedural knowledge, and to allow space for other important aspects of education. We need to scrutinise the purpose of what we are learning for a life well lived.

Greater prominence needs to be given to schools as well-funded social centres, as well as to preparation for citizenship for all children and young people. This will require a view of cultural literacy that allows our pupils to engage in an informed manner at national and international level, but also affords them the time and space to explore their own heritage and history. Their engagement in these matters cannot be purely intellectual. They must be empowered. We must work in solidarity with the poorest and marginalised. We must do good.

A new leadership imperative

When educating with purpose, leadership is of paramount importance: "Leaders manage meaning for a group" (Goleman et al, 2002). Leadership is contingent on values, knowledge and relationships. The values we hold to as leaders – and *what* we value – give us purpose and perspective. Our understanding of works, theories and bodies of knowledge informs and guides us. Relationships help to create influence and enable successful enactment. Values, knowledge and relationships collectively form the hinterland we use when making and implementing decisions. Our belief system, prior knowledge and experiences are the basis for future actions.

The decade ahead requires a more collaborative profession, internally supportive and more able and enabled to work effectively with others. We succeed through unity. This will help to move leadership from the transactional to the transformational. Our assessments need to provide powerful feedback loops to inform improvement.

Speaking in February 2020 at the Headteachers' Roundtable Summit, I talked about a decade untouched. Little did I realise how important the profession's collective agency, wisdom and sense of service would be in the months ahead. Although this decade still has a long way to run, it has now been deeply and profoundly touched. The impact of the Covid-19 pandemic and the seismic response to the killing of George Floyd might, through great tragedy and suffering, bring forth a more just, peaceful and compassionate world. A world that will no longer accept a life well lived for the few, but demands it for all.

We must sing into existence this future, one that will serve our children, young people and communities well.

References

Afzal, N. (2020) *The Prosecutor: one man's pursuit of justice for the voiceless,* London: Ebury Publishing

Allen, R. (2019) "Careering towards a curriculum crash?", *Becky Allen* (blog), tinyurl.com/y9spcmkc

Arnold, M. (1864) "The function of criticism at the present time", Fortnightly Review, tinyurl.com/ycss9dsq

Arnold, M. (1869) *Culture and Anarchy: an essay in political and social criticism.* Reproduction of the original library book by Google

Biesta, G. (2015) "What is education for? On good education, teacher judgement, and educational professionalism", *European Journal of Education*, 50:1

Block, P. (2008) *Community: the structure of belonging*, Berrett-Koehler

Chalke, S. (2016) "Inspired to take a positive approach against extremism", *Schools for Human Flourishing*, pp.44-48, London: SSAT, Woodard Schools and Church of England Education Office

Coe, R. (2013) "Improving education: a triumph of hope over experience", inaugural lecture of Professor Robert Coe, Durham University, cem.org/attachments/publications/improvingeducation2013.pdf

Coffield, F. (2019) "Coffield: 7 problems with inspections Ofsted must fix", *Tes*, tinyurl.com/yddxahsf

Counsell, C. (2018) "Taking curriculum seriously", *Impact: Journal of the Chartered College of Teaching*, 4, pp. 6-9, tinyurl.com/rcl94u7

Crehan, L. (2016) *Cleverlands*, London: Unbound

Dubiel, J. (2014) "Learning and development: assessment – measuring up", *Nursery World*, tinyurl.com/ybq97gvs

Freire, P. (1974) *Education: The Practice of Freedom*, London: Writers and Readers Publishing Cooperative

Freire, P. (2017) *Pedagogy of the Oppressed*. Penguin Classics (the original translation into English was published in 1970)

Fried, J. and Heinemeier Hansson, D. (2018) *It Doesn't Have to be Crazy at Work*, London: HarperCollins Publishers

Goleman, D., Boyatzis, R. and McKee, A. (2002) *Primal Leadership*, Boston: Harvard Business School Press

Hattie, J. (2009) *Visible Learning: a synthesis of over 800 meta-analyses relating to achievement*, Abingdon, Oxon: Routledge

Headteachers' Roundtable. (2016) *The Alternative Green Paper: schools that enable all to thrive and flourish*, London: Schools Week, tinyurl.com/y99wc5q3

Heath, D. (2020) *Upstream: how to solve problems before they happen*, London: Penguin Random House UK

Hirsch Jr, E.D. (1988) *Cultural Literacy*, New York: Vintage Books

Hirsch Jr, E.D. (1999) *The Schools We Need and Why We Don't Have Them*, New York: Anchor Books/Doubleday

Kingsnorth, S. (2019) "Forget Finland. Could Estonia help to reverse our dire results?", *Medium*, tinyurl.com/y6yx28tn

Logan, P. M. (2012) "On Culture: Matthew Arnold's *Culture and Anarchy*, 1869", *BRANCH* (Britain, Representation and Nineteenth-Century History), tinyurl.com/ydghby6w

Lough, C. (2020) "Dylan Wiliam: 'Immoral' to teach 'too full' curriculum", *Tes*, tinyurl.com/y9pd69w2

Major, L.E. (2019) "SSAT National Conference 2019: conference speakers", SSAT, ssatuk.co.uk/nc19/speakers, accessed 22 June 2020

McInerney, L. (2020) "Education was never schools' sole focus. The coronavirus pandemic has proved it", *The Guardian*, tinyurl.com/qujqrty

Ofsted. (2019) *School Inspection Handbook: handbook for inspecting schools in England under section 5 of the Education Act 2005*, Ofsted, Crown copyright

Organisation for Economic Co-operation and Development. (2004) *Background OECD Papers: The Schooling Scenarios*, OECD Publishing, tinyurl.com/yc5cs9ka

Organisation for Economic Co-operation and Development. (2019) *PISA 2018 Results (Volume III): what school life means for students' lives*, OECD Publishing, doi.org/10.1787/acd78851-en

Plaister, N. and Thomson, D. (2019) "Looking at the London effect five years on: part two", FFT Education Datalab, tinyurl.com/yckmvfp3

Postman, N. (1994) *The Disappearance of Childhood*, New York: Vintage Books

PwC. (2020) *Navigating the Rising Tide of Uncertainty: 23rd annual global CEO survey*, PwC Global, tinyurl.com/vtxlzya

Robinson, M. (2018) "Curriculum: an offer of what the best might be", *Impact: Journal of the Chartered College of Teaching*, 4, pp.13-15, tinyurl.com/y9ovzy94

Rohr, R. (2020) "The patterns that are always true", Center for Action and Contemplation, tinyurl.com/y9uled72

Sentamu, J. (2016) "Nurturing the heart, mind and soul: the spiritual context of education", *Schools for Human Flourishing*, pp.84-90, London: SSAT, Woodard Schools and Church of England Education Office

Sherrington, T. (2018) "What is a 'knowledge-rich' curriculum?", *Impact: Journal of the Chartered College of Teaching*, 4, pp.19-20, tinyurl.com/ycnrfmg8

SSAT. (2015) *Redesigning Schooling: A Vision for Education – beyond five-year policy cycles*, London: SSAT, tinyurl.com/ya4dzsbc

Sylva, K., Melhuish, E., Sammons, P., Siraj-Blatchford, I. and Taggart, B. (2004) *The Effective Provision of Pre-School Education (EPPE) Project: findings from pre-school to end of Key Stage 1*, Sure Start, tinyurl.com/yb9kdn9b

Teacher Tapp. (2018) "What Teacher Tapped this week #60 – 19th November 2018", Teacher Tapp, tinyurl.com/y73qkcm6

White, B. (2019) "The 'wicked problem' of school improvement", *Walden Education* (blog), tinyurl.com/y88xw5ay

White, J. (2018) "The weakness of 'powerful knowledge'", *London Review of Education*, 16:2, pp.325–335, doi.org/10.18546/LRE.16.2.11

Wiliam, D. (2013) *Redesigning Schooling: Principled Curriculum Design*, SSAT, tinyurl.com/y9eeb4eu

Wiliam, D. (2018) *Creating the Schools Our Children Need*, West Palm Beach, Florida: Learning Sciences International

Williams, R. (2011) *The Long Revolution*, Cardigan: Parthian (first published in 1961)

Willingham, D.T. (2017) *The Reading Mind: a cognitive approach to understanding how the mind reads*, San Francisco: Jossey-Bass

Winston, R. (2003) *The Human Mind*, London: BBC Books

Young, M. (2014) *The Curriculum and the Entitlement to Knowledge*, Cambridge Assessment Network, tinyurl.com/y8udwl6z

Young, M. (2015) "Unleashing the power of knowledge for all", *Spiked*, tinyurl.com/ybllyz5j